A LIFE OF THEIR OWN

An Indian Family in Latin America

A LIFE OF THEIR OWN

An Indian Family in Latin America

Text and Photographs by

Aylette Jenness & Lisa W. Kroeber

DRAWINGS BY SUSAN VOTAW

Thomas Y. Crowell Company   New York

BY AYLETTE JENNESS

Along the Niger River
An African Way of Life

BY AYLETTE JENNESS AND LISA W. KROEBER

A Life of Their Own
An Indian Family in Latin America

Library of Congress Cataloging in Publication Data
Jenness, Aylette. A life of their own.
Bibliography: p. Includes index.
1. Indians of Central America—Guatemala—Social
life and customs—Juvenile literature   2. Guatemala—
Social life and customs—Juvenile literature.
I. Kroeber, Lisa, joint author.   II. Votaw, Susan.
III. Title. F1465.3.S62J45   972.81′004′97   75-15964
ISBN 0-690-00572-5
1   2   3   4   5   6   7   8   9   10

This book is dedicated to the Hernandez family and to their friends and neighbors in San Antonio —especially Padre Frank and David Lopez and his daughters, Maximina and Marta. They put up with our insistent presence, our endless and sometimes foolish questions, our cameras and tape recorders, our jarring sense of time, and our long noses—with friendliness, interest, tolerance, and patience. They welcomed us into their lives with much pride; we feel ourselves fortunate to share this experience with our readers.

We are grateful to Patsy Asch, Sam Bowles, Jim Cannon, Delores DeCarli, Marilyn Kriegel, Ted Kroeber, Phylis Morrison, and David Rush, who were most important to us as we wrote this book. They gave a lot of their time and energy—reading the manuscript and raising issues and discussing them. They were always available when we needed them, and their participation enriched us as well as this book.

In addition, Bonnie Rottier and Liza Kroeber shared our Guatemala home; Duane Beeson sent a new tape recorder to us in Guatemala when ours broke; D'Arcy Marsh took "author" pictures; and David Drake introduced us to the Hernandezes.

We feel fortunate that so many friends involved themselves in the making of this book.

Contents

Foreword

We had many purposes in mind as we wrote this book; some are obvious, but others may not be. Our primary goal is to describe some aspects of contemporary Indian life in Latin America. The first section, *"Del libro*—About the Book," is designed to lead the United States reader into the Indian world with us, to heighten his or her sense of the reality of the Indians, and to give the reader insights into cultural differences and the problems and pleasures these create. In *"La familia Hernandez*—The Hernandez Family," through familiarity with the Hernandezes and their daily activities, the reader learns about Indian culture, craftwork, agriculture, trade, transportation, education, local government, public health, and religion. In *"Taller*—Workshop," we suggest related experiments and projects that the reader can do to gain experiential understanding of Indian life, in either a school or a home setting. Some of these activities are designed to be done by a single child, others by a group; all are planned to use widely available materials and environments.

For school use, we encourage the beginning student of Spanish to find understanding and pleasure in the language, through our gradual introduction of generally useful Spanish words in the text, and a listing of them in the short Vocabulary at the end of the book. Specific information needed for a social-studies project can easily be tapped by using the Index. Those interested in the cultural heritage of various Spanish Americans will find relevant material throughout the book.

Another purpose of ours is to give the reader some understanding of a particular field of adult work—that of researching and writing a book—which we feel is important in an era when children are isolated from the adult work world. *"Del libro"* provides the reader with some information about a field he or she might want to be part of some day, and also suggests ways of learning and working that can be used by a child immediately. Our attitudes and techniques—observing, learning about and documenting things that interested us—can be used by anyone, anywhere. We hope some readers may be sparked to do writing and/or photography projects on their own—drawing on their family or community life, or experiences in places they may visit.

In addition, we think that understanding the methods of mass communications is of vital importance to children today, and we hope that our brief account in the first section of how this book was made will provide some useful knowledge of one medium.

Finally, we hope that we have shown through our own experiences and the outcome of them that learning and working can be, even when difficult, joyful and exciting experiences.

NORTH AMERICA

Atlantic Ocean

GUATEMALA

CENTRAL AMERICA

Pacific Ocean

MEXICO

BRITISH
HONDURAS

GUATEMALA

Sumpango
Antigua
San Antonio
Aguas Calientes

Guatemala City

EL SALVADOR

SOUTH AMERICA

Del libro—

About the Book

Many of the mountains in Guatemala are old volcanoes. Their tall cones rise in regular sweeping curves, one after another, all across this small country. A few are still active. Smoking craters erupt from time to time, shaking the land, spilling rivers of lava down their sides and into the warm green valleys. Mayan Indians have lived in these highlands for centuries, and that's why we went there. We wanted to make a book about how one group of Latin American Indians lives today. There was one big problem: we didn't know any.

The first thing we did was to find an apartment in Antigua, an old town in the highlands. The apartment was part of a coffee plantation, and inside its high thick walls, we shared our garden with a bird who sang like a rusty wind-up toy and with several large and fancy insects. We made friends with Samuel, age eleven, and Elena, age thirteen, who did much of the work in the apartments.

We spent our first few days exploring Antigua. We walked for hours and hours in the big indoor market, where all kinds of things were sold—from a padlock to a glass of fresh goat's milk,

The volcano Fuego, surrounded by morning clouds

from a hair ribbon to a hundred-pound sack of corn. The market was so huge and so crowded that we often got separated—but could always find one another again because of our height. At five feet six inches, we were tall enough to spot one another by looking over the heads of all the people, as though we were giraffes. The Indians' style of dress and the sound of their languages were exciting and strange to us. They seemed friendly, but very different from ourselves; we wondered if we would ever understand enough of their lives to write a book.

Then we went to see a Peace Corps language specialist. A friend in the United States had suggested we talk to him about our project. He offered to introduce us to his friends the Hernandezes, an Indian family who lived in the nearby village of San Antonio. He said that he would meet us the next day in the *parque central*—the central park—in Antigua, where Flora Hernandez and her seventeen-year-old daughter, Marylena, would be selling their cloth. We were delighted. We raced home to make and practice a greeting speech for the Hernandezes. This was the first of many times we rehearsed what we were going to say in Spanish. We found that if we planned our conversations and questions in advance, we were more likely to understand what was being said—by everyone.

Our first meeting with Flora and Marylena Hernandez went smoothly. So did our speech. We told them we would like to spend a lot of time with them, asking questions, taking photographs, and learning about their lives, and that we wanted

to make a book from the information we col-
lected. They spent some time discussing our ideas
with each other in Cakchiquel, their native language, smiled, and then told us in their limited
Spanish that they would be pleased to help us.
We were grateful and very happy. They suggested that we come to their home in San Antonio
the following day. Flora said, *"Les esperamos a
las ocho de la mañana."* "We expect you at eight
in the morning."

We walked to the bus very early the next morning because we had already discovered that buses
in Guatemala follow a schedule all their own;
they leave *ahorita*—just now—which can mean
in one minute or maybe in one hour. In Antigua
the bus for San Antonio left *ahorita* and also
whenever it was full. It was about the size of a
Volkswagen van and was considered full when
more than twenty people had climbed in. After
a bumpy ten-minute ride over dirt roads, we arrived in San Antonio.

Following the directions we had been given,
we walked down a winding, fence-lined lane and
knocked on the gate of the Hernandezes' compound—their living space—promptly at eight
o'clock. No answer. We knocked again. Much
scuffling and moving around inside. We waited.
Finally Marylena opened the gate, and with a
look of great surprise, said, *"¡Ya están aquí!
Pasan adelante."* "You're here already! Come in."

We stepped through the gate in the cornstalk
fence, and Marylena introduced us to her father,
Hipolitó, her brother Arnoldo, and her sister
Evelia. She asked us to sit down, and we began

to look around us at the Hernandezes' home. Their property was a long, narrow plot enclosed by a high fence made of cornstalks. Several small, cornstalk-walled rooms with thatched roofs were clustered near the center of the lot. The large work area where we sat was roofed with aluminum; most of the rest of the compound was open to the sky. The air smelled of flowers, of wood fires, and of food cooking. The floor was packed earth, which felt cool to our feet, and there were fruit trees, vines, and bushes growing everywhere.

Flora joined us, and as we talked, it became clear that we had found the way to make our book. We would tell something of what it's like to be part of the Indian population of Latin America by telling about the life of the Hernandez family. It seemed so easy. The fact that neither we nor the Hernandezes spoke Spanish fluently didn't bother us a bit. Our best language, of course, was English; theirs was Cakchiquel. We didn't realize how easy it would be to misunderstand the language and to confuse ourselves—and the Hernandezes as well.

Our first experience that day should have warned us. Marylena had obviously been surprised when we arrived at eight in the morning, for she had said "*¡Ya están aquí!*"

It was a phrase we were to hear often, since we were never quite able to get used to the indefinite way that Guatemalans handled time. Once we planned to go with the Hernandez family to a *fiesta* in the town of Sumpango. They said they would meet us in the *parque central* in Antigua at two in the afternoon. We arrived just before two. We waited. And waited. Finally at four in the afternoon we gave up, thinking something had happened to them. We were walking out of the *parque* when we saw them get off a bus. They came over to us with smiles and greetings, and said with astonishment, "*¡Ya están aquí!*"

We finally decided that our more definite use of time and schedules was something we had learned in the United States and it was not popular in Guatemala. The Hernandezes, who always wanted to be very polite, would agree to a meeting time, or even suggest one, because we seemed to expect it. Then they would arrive when their chores were done and they were ready.

Muy lejos—very far—was another phrase that seemed strange to us for a long while. When we asked Hipolitó if we could go and photograph him farming, he said, "*No es posible; está muy lejos.*" "It is not possible; it is very far." That had already been the answer to several of our requests, and this time it made no sense. His fields of *chiles*—peppers—were right near San Antonio. How could they be *muy lejos*? At last we figured out that *muy lejos* was a simple and polite way of saying that what we wanted was difficult or inconvenient for him. It was easier to say *muy lejos* than to go into a long explanation, which we might not understand, of why it was inconvenient. This phrase was also a good cover for situations that people felt were too personal to discuss.

We never discovered what was *muy lejos* about going to Hipolitó's fields. Perhaps he would have

been embarrassed to take two *gringas*—foreign women—to his fields, a man's working place. At any rate, we had to settle for detailed interviews with Hipolitó about farming, and visits to other farmers' fields.

We took that bumpy bus ride from Antigua to San Antonio almost every day, and spent most of our time in the Hernandezes' compound. We photographed, asked questions, and made tape recordings. Flora and Marylena were delighted to show us their weaving—how to wind yarn into balls and how to thread the warping board in preparation for setting up a loom. They were patient and skilled teachers, and we were very slow, awkward students. The least of our problems was that we stood too tall for the warping board. Mainly, we had none of the rhythm and grace that comes from hundreds of hours of practice. Flora and Marylena giggled and laughed as they watched us struggle with tasks they considered as easy as breathing. We laughed, too, and at the same time developed a great admiration for their skill.

After Flora and Marylena had shown us how they wove their clothes, they wanted to see how we would look wearing them. Compared to our jeans and shirts, their garments felt rich and heavy to us. They had to help us wind and drape the *falda*—skirt. Once the tight *cinturón*—belt— was in place, they braided bright ribbons into our hair and stood back to view the result. They seemed very pleased. When we took off the beautiful clothes, we forgot the hair ribbons and wore them home on the bus. We noticed that the other

Top: A man talks with Aylette about planting corn.
Middle: Marylena teaches Aylette to use a swift.
Bottom: Aylette practices at the warping board.

passengers smiled at us more than usual, but we didn't find out the reason until we arrived home. Then it was our turn to smile.

The Hernandez family always shared their midday dinner with us. At eleven thirty Flora or a helper began to cook *tortillas*—corn pancakes—and Marylena ground the *frijoles negros*—black beans—which had been simmering all morning. We helped set the table, and added whatever contribution we had brought. Hard-boiled eggs, soda pop, and white rolls were favorites. Once we brought fresh plums, which we thought would be a great treat. Everyone dutifully took one, then quietly dropped it somewhere out of sight. They were too polite to refuse anything we offered—even if it was something they didn't like.

When the meal was ready, the whole family would sit down together to eat and to talk about the events of the morning. Sometimes even we had items of local news we could share—that we had seen Padre Frank, the village priest, blessing a new house, or that we had bumped into Flora's sister-in-law Estrella selling cloth in Antigua. Talking in Spanish without our rehearsed speeches and questions was difficult—but it was then that we felt most like part of the family as we laughed together and learned about one another.

Flora and Hipolitó were amazed at the idea of two women traveling alone, and obviously thought it strange that we weren't at home with our families. The information that one of us had no children was very startling. Marylena and Ev-

Top: Marylena and Flora braid Aylette's hair.
Bottom: Lisa takes photographs in the *cocina*—kitchen.

elia were intrigued by the fact that one of us did not have pierced ears. In San Antonio, soon after a girl is born, her ears are pierced. Flora told us that the baby does not cry if the piercing is done during a new moon. One day at dinner Flora commented on our noses—long and pointed compared to theirs. She said she was told as a child that in the United States parents put a clothespin on their childrens' noses to make them grow longer. She laughed, admitting she had believed it then but didn't now.

Conversations at noon often blended into interviews. These were long, quiet, exploring talks. Sometimes it was a struggle to find the right question. Sometimes it was a peaceful time, a sharing of memories and of explanations about our different lives. Other times it was a period of great confusion—for instance, when Hipolitó was trying to tell us about *barriletes*. We had been asking about games and recreation, and he said to us, "*Cuando mucho aire, hacemos barriletes.*"

Well, we knew *aire* meant "air" and *hacemos* meant "we make," but we didn't know what *barriletes* were. We tried using the small dictionary we always carried with us. Because the Spanish *b* and *v* sound the same, we looked up both *barriletes* and varriletes. No luck. Then we tried a possible verb—*bolar* or *volar*—and guessed that whatever the word was, it had to do with flying. "*Cuando mucho aire—barriletes,*" Hipolitó repeated.

We said, "*¿Triquitraques?*" "Firecrackers?"

Much laughter. No, *barriletes*.

We said, "*¿Aeroplanos?*" "Airplanes?"

Flora winds thread as she talks about her childhood.

More laughter. No, *barriletes*.

Later, when we listened to our tape recording of this conversation, we counted Hipolitó saying, "*Cuando mucho aire—barriletes*," nine times before we finally figured out that he was talking about kites, and we said, "*Oh, sí, barriletes*."

We had talked so long about *barriletes* and seemed to know so little about them, that Hipolitó offered to show us how they were constructed. Several days later we spent the morning watching the family making *barriletes*, even though it wasn't really the windy time of year. When we were leaving, the Hernandezes gave us the *barriletes* to take home.

The first person who saw us walking along the road carrying kites laughed and said, "*No es el tiempo para barriletes*." We smiled. A block later, a group of young men saw us, and after laughing quite a bit, said, "*No es el tiempo para barriletes*." Seeing us with *barriletes* at the wrong time of year seemed very strange to them. We might as well have been eating petunias with chopsticks.

Finally we arrived back at our apartment. Samuel, who worked there, greeted us, saying seriously, "*¡Oh, señoritas, no es el tiempo para barriletes!*"

When at last it was time for us to return to our jobs and families in the United States, we found that leaving was hard. We'd made some friends; we no longer felt like strangers. We'd made some mistakes; we'd laughed about them and learned from them. And we'd grown fond of the people of San Antonio. On our last day there we brought the Hernandezes small going-away presents—a flashlight for Arnoldo, earrings for Evelia, perfume for Marylena. We were even more tongue-tied than usual when we discovered that they had weavings for us with our names brocaded into the now familiar San Antonio patterns.

Working on the book in the United States was far different from living it in Guatemala. How were we to choose two hundred photographs for the book from the nearly four thousand we had taken? How were we to make a clear story out of hours of tape recordings, sheafs of notes, and folders of drawings? How were we to write about the startling noise of fireworks, the smell of fresh *tortillas*, the peaceful atmosphere in the Hernandez home, when one of us was in a city apartment in Massachusetts and the other in a house in California? We were able to get together to print the photographs, and the Hernandez family began to appear on paper—a first step. When we were apart again, our phone bills soared, and we made many trips to the mailbox with drafts of the text and lists of questions: "Dear Lisa, What is the *enfermera*'s last name? I can't remember." "Dear Aylette, Please check Hipolitó's tape on farming. How many *cuerdas* does he have?" At last the time came for the completed text and photographs to go to the editor in New York.

At the publishing company a whole new job began. Our editor read the manuscript and made suggestions for improving it. A copy editor checked it very carefully for grammar, spelling, and accuracy of information. A designer planned the layout, page by page, making the photographs and the text match each other.

At the printers, huge presses inked many pages at a time on big sheets of paper. Other machines automatically cut, sorted, and folded the pages, and still others bound them into—a book! Then all the thousands of copies were shipped to schools, libraries, bookstores—and to you.

The Hernandezes and their neighbors are still living and working in San Antonio, but a part of their lives is in these pages. This book is in your hands now, and it's up to you to decide how you want to use it. You can read it from beginning to end. You can look only at the pictures, and if you want, you can read the captions to find out a little more. If you're doing a school project, and you want information on topics such as agriculture, transportation, or education, use the Index to find the pages you particularly want to read. If you're studying Spanish, you can add to your knowledge by learning the Spanish words in the text. There's a Vocabulary at the back to help you with this. The third section, *Taller*—Workshop, suggests some experiences and projects you may want to try out. Whatever you do with it, we hope you find the book useful and fun.

We and the people you'll see here—the Hernandez family, their neighbors, Padre Frank, Alicia the *enfermera* (what *is* her last name?)—all of us had a good time living and working on this story. As Marylena Hernandez said when we first knocked on the door, *"Pasan adelante."*

La familia Hernandez—

The Hernandez Family

Pasado a presente—
Past to Present

The village of San Antonio lies in a long narrow valley ringed by steep hills. The dark blue cones of three volcanoes—Agua, Fuego, and Acatenango—rise tall behind the hills. A thin column of smoke rising from Fuego is a reminder that volcanic eruptions—and earthquakes—have destroyed farms and villages here in the past, and may again.

Evelia, Arnoldo, and Marylena Hernandez have lived in San Antonio all their lives. So have their parents, Flora and Hipolitó, and so did their parents and their parents' parents and their parents' parents' parents for as far back in time as anyone can remember. It is a very old village. San Antonio is laid out like villages in Spain, with a large open space—a *plazuela*—in the center. The church dominates the *plazuela* here as it has for more than four hundred years. Opposite the church is a *pila,* a large fountain with many basins where the women of San Antonio draw their water and wash their clothes. On the other two sides of the *plazuela* are the public elementary school, the mayor's office, and the jail.

From the *plazuela* a network of roads and lanes spreads out in all directions, closely lined with the compounds of the five thousand people who live here. Some compounds are large, some small, but all are similar in design to the Hernandezes'. Scattered among them are several *tiendas*—small stores—where Flora can buy soap, candles, and some packaged foods. There is a tailor's shop. There is a new *puesto de salud*—health clinic. There is a *carpintería*—carpenter's shop—where a friend of Hipolitó's makes furniture for the living and coffins for the dead. There are the *molinos* —mills—where Flora and her neighbors take their corn to be ground by machine each morning.

Almost all the people of San Antonio are Indian. Like the Hernandezes, they speak Cakchiquel, follow many Indian customs, and wear Indian clothes. How does it happen that this village, laid out so exactly like a Spanish town, belongs to Indians? The story is an old one, far older than the village itself.

More than a thousand years ago, ancestors of the Hernandezes were part of an elaborate Mayan civilization in Mexico and Central America. These Indians built huge stone temples and ceremonial centers that towered above the tropical forests. Their rulers and religious leaders developed the sciences of astronomy and mathematics to a high degree. Mayan artisans made beautiful cloth, pottery, jewelry, wood and stone carvings.

Four hundred and fifty years ago bands of Spanish soldiers sailed across the Atlantic Ocean, landed on the shores of Central America, and proceeded to conquer the Indians. The Spaniards were greedy for gold; they cared little about the Indians or their culture. They systematically killed the Indian leaders and quickly wrecked the civilization of centuries.

The Spaniards soon found that there was not nearly as much gold in Guatemala as they had hoped. They thought, however, that they might still grow rich by forcing the Indians to work for them, producing food and handcrafts that could be shipped to Spain.

And so the Spaniards laid out villages and towns like San Antonio. They made the Indians clear the land for *plazuelas* and build churches and public buildings. They baptized the Indians in the Roman Catholic faith, gave them Spanish names, and told them to settle in the villages. The Spaniards took the most fertile and level land for their large profitable plantations, forcing the Indians to work on them. The Indians were left the steep hillsides on which to raise their own food.

And so it continues today. Though Guatemala is independent from Spain, and her people are technically all equal citizens, the descendants of the Spaniards are the very small, powerful, wealthy class that owns most of the land. The descendants of the native Indians form a large part of the poorer class.

The Hernandezes and their neighbors raise vegetables and fruits on the hillsides, just as their ancestors did more than four hundred years ago. The women of San Antonio weave fine strong cloth, using patterns that go back to their Mayan forebears. Outsiders have brought new ideas, which have blended with the old. Day after day, year after year, the people of San Antonio follow their accustomed work—slowly, steadily, evenly.

Quehaceres—
Chores

For the Hernandezes each day begins early; there is much work to be done, and every hour of light is needed. The family begins to wake when the first blue light of dawn dimly illuminates their compound—the trees and plants at the high back end of the lot, the rooms clustered near the center, and the large work space near the front gate. The two sleeping rooms—*cuartos para dormir*—are small, enclosed, and dark. The walls are of strong cornstalks, lined with woven rush mats. The roofs are of thick grass thatch. The family sleeps here warmly wrapped in woolen blankets made high in the mountains, the sheep-raising part of Guatemala. Flora and Hipolitó rise first from their bed of wooden boards covered with a rush mat. Arnoldo and Evelia, sharing a bed in the same room, stir drowsily.

Marylena, in her own room, stretches and gets up, reaching for her clothes. She first puts on her white cotton underblouse, with its crisp band of embroidery around the neck and down the front. Next she pulls over her head one of her *huipiles* —Indian blouses. She wraps about herself the eighteen-foot length of striped woolen cloth which is her *falda*—skirt. Holding the heavy mass

Top: A snug bedroom in the Hernandezes' compound.
Bottom: Flora feeds the family's chicken.

of *falda* skillfully in place, she winds her embroidered *cinturón* tightly around and around her waist, and firmly tucks in the end. Then she slowly combs her long black hair until there is not a snarl in it, and binds it with an elastic. She puts on one of her necklaces, and slips her feet into the everyday shoes she wears at home.

Each member of the family rolls up his or her blanket neatly, and begins the day. Each person has particular chores to do before breakfast and sets quietly to work, talking to the others a little bit, sleepily.

Flora, still yawning, smoothing back her hair, walks up the path to the back of the compound, past the pits that have been dug to hold trash, past Hipolitó's seedbed for *chile* plants. A *gallina*, tied by the orange trees and *café* bushes, clucks impatiently as Flora throws her a handful of corn and some green leaves. Chicken is a rarity in the Hernandez family, for meat of any kind is expensive. The Hernandezes bought this hen at the market in Antigua and are fattening it for the christening feast of one of Flora's nieces. The Hernandezes' toilet, a pit covered with a raised wooden seat and surrounded on three sides by woven mat walls, is at this end of the compound. Flora checks the basket on the ground nearby to make sure that there are some newspapers to use for toilet paper.

Marylena's first morning chore is to tidy the compound. Now seventeen years old, she no longer needs to be reminded about this by her parents. She sweeps out the *cocina*—kitchen—then the *baño*, where the family bathes, and near the front of the compound, the main working area,

Top: Woven rush mats enclose the Hernandezes' toilet.
Bottom: Marylena sweeps the compound's earthen floor.

a large space roofed over with sheets of aluminum. Hipolitó sprinkles the ground with water as soon as Marylena has swept this area. The cool water, quickly absorbed into the hard-packed earth, prevents dust from rising during the heat of the day.

Arnoldo and Evelia, faces and hands scrubbed, dressed in clean clothes for school, use the early morning light to finish their homework here. Hipolitó stops his work for a moment to look at Arnoldo's paper. "I will read it over in a minute," Hipolitó says. They both laugh at the joke; Hipolitó was able to go to school for only a few years when he was a boy, and Arnoldo, at twelve, is able to read, write, and figure arithmetic far better than his father can.

Beside this main working area is the *galera de imagenes*, a large dim chapel room, one side of which is used for storage. As is common in Catholic families all over the world, the Hernandezes have a special place for prayer in their home. Theirs has framed prints of Jesus, Joseph, and Mary, and the Hernandezes' favorite saints, hanging above a large table spread with a cloth. Marylena checks the fresh flowers she keeps in front of the table, removing dead blossoms and adding water to the vases. As she finishes saying a short prayer, there is a knock on the outside door of the house.

Marylena goes to answer it. "*Shak*," she says, greeting in Cakchiquel the neighbor who stands there with a basket of tomatoes on her head. "Yes," she says, "we need to buy some today. Two pounds will be enough."

The neighbor has a one-pound brass weight, the

only one she owns, and an equal weight of lemons in the pan on one side of her balance scale. She begins to fill the other pan with tomatoes until the two sides are evenly balanced. Marylena smiles and nods, holding out her basket. She pays the old woman, saying quietly, *"Matiosh"*—thank you in Cakchiquel. As she takes the *tomates* to the *cocina*, she passes her mother preparing to go out to get water.

Water is not piped to homes in San Antonio, so all the villagers collect the rainwater that falls almost daily from May until October. The Hernandezes have attached a gutter along the edge of the metal roof of the *cocina*, and this drains into a barrel under its end. They use this rainwater for washing and cleaning, but even during the rainy season, it is not enough to supply all the household needs. Besides, for cooking and drinking the Hernandezes prefer the cool clear water from the public *pila*—fountain—closest to their

Top: A neighbor sells Marylena some *tomates*.
Bottom: Flora sets off for water.

home. Water is piped here, and to other *pilas* in San Antonio, from a river near the village.

Flora quickly rolls her *tsute* up into a doughnut-shaped pad and puts it on her head. The *tsute* is a cloth used by Indian women to carry food and babies, to wrap around themselves in cold weather, to shade their heads when the sun is hot, and to fold and drape decoratively over their shoulders. Like women in many other parts of the world—South America, Africa, Asia—Flora has learned since early childhood to carry almost all her burdens on her head, leaving her arms free. She puts the *tsute* on her head, the empty clay water jug on top, and opening the wooden gate of the compound, steps down into the lane outside her house.

After she has carried the fresh water she needs back to the compound, she returns to the *pila* to do the family laundry. She does this every day, for the Hernandezes do not have many changes of clothing, and they like to be freshly dressed at all times. The *pila* has many concrete basins for washing clothes. Flora puts the clothes, one garment at a time, in a basin and then scoops up clean water from the fountain to pour over them. She scrubs the clothes with soap, then rubs them gently over the concrete of the basin. When she is ready to rinse, she dips her bowl into the *pila* again, being careful not to let any soapsuds fall, since the *pila* supplies drinking and cooking water for everyone. She pours the bowl of clean water over the clothes, holding it so that her hand is rinsed at the same time. The water in the basin drains through a hole, and is carried away underground.

Top: Public fountains supply the village with water.
Middle and bottom: Flora does the family laundry here, too, washing the clothes in the basins of the *pila*.

At the *pila*, Flora has a chance to chat with her neighbors, to exchange news, to learn about the latest happenings in the neighborhood. The women talk in quiet tones, tease, laugh with each other, commiserate over problems.

They talk about the *puesto de salud*, the health clinic, which has been recently built in San Antonio. The *enfermera*—nurse—wants to vaccinate all the children against whooping cough. Some of the women are wary of Alicia Cajia, the *enfermera*. She seems nice, but after all she is a *ladino*. The women remember many bad experiences with *ladinos*, as they call the non-Indian Guatemalans. Some of the older women are suspicious of the inoculations, saying that they make the children sore and feverish. How can that be good? The younger mothers say yes, that's true, but the children do not get whooping cough if they have had the vaccination. Everyone knows that many Indians die of this sickness every year. Yes, perhaps the new medicine is a good idea.

One of the women talks about the new workroom her family has just finished making. They have sent a message to the nearby village of Dueñas where Padre Frank lives, asking him to bless the building. Though he has only recently been appointed priest for several villages in this area, many people already know and like him. It is clear that he doesn't look down on Indians, as most *ladinos* do.

On the way back from the *pila*, Flora notices that the butcher has hung up his red flag to show that beef is ready for sale. Earlier in the morning several cows were killed in the small slaughter-

Top: At the *pila* Flora chats with her neighbors.
Middle: A little girl practices washing clothes.
Bottom: The village butcher cuts a piece of meat.

house on the edge of town. Since the butcher has no refrigeration, those who want beef that day get it as soon as possible so that it will be fresh. Flora decides to return and buy a small piece. It costs fifty *centavos*—fifty cents in United States money. At this price the Hernandezes can occasionally afford to have a vegetable stew or soup flavored with meat.

While Flora is at the butcher, one of the most important of the morning chores has begun—*tortilla* making. The Hernandez family eats four pounds of corn in *tortillas* every day of the year. All over the world people who have little money can buy only small amounts of foods rich in protein—eggs, meat, poultry, fish—so they eat a large amount of starchy foods, which are much cheaper. In the Orient people eat rice, and in the United States, bread and potatoes. With the Hernandez family, as with most Latin Americans, the making of *tortillas* is as regular, as expectable, as the morning itself.

Kernels of corn are set to soak in water overnight; then early in the morning, they are boiled with a lump of white, flaky lime, which softens the tough outer coverings. After it is cooked, the corn is drained, washed, and carried to the *molino*, one of the small, electric-powered mills owned and run by San Antonio men. These mills save an hour or two every day for the women who would otherwise laboriously grind the grain by rolling it with a stone cylinder on a stone slab, the *metate*. However, the *molino* does not make the corn quite fine enough for good *tortillas*, so it must still be briefly reground at home. Since the

Top: Flora wraps the beef she has bought.
Middle: The red flag shows that the butcher has meat.
Bottom: Corn is soaked and drained, then ground.

Hernandezes are so busy with their trade in cloth —weaving and selling—they often hire neighbors to do some of their housework for them. This old widow, her face as worn as her *huipil*, sometimes takes their corn to the *molino* and makes the *tortillas*. She is glad to get some food in return.

The Hernandezes' *cocina*—kitchen—has low walls of adobe, or sun-dried brick, and above them, cornstalk fencing. It is furnished with a couple of low chairs and a tightly screened cabinet, holding dishes and the few utensils they need —a knife, a food mill, a large spoon for cooking and smaller ones for eating. Since they do not have any refrigeration, they do not store food which would spoil. In the corner is a fireplace of three stones on which to balance the *comal*, the pottery griddle for cooking *tortillas*. Beside it is the iron tripod on which is set, nearly every day, the pot in which *frijoles negros*—black beans— are cooked.

The early morning air is cool, and the old woman is glad to have the warmth of the fire she has made. It is quiet in the compound, quiet in the *cocina*; there is little noise except for the crackle of the fire and the even, steady mushing sound of corn ground against stone. The widow takes great care to keep everything clean, to avoid getting any earth from the floor onto the meal. When she has ground enough corn on the *metate* for a platter of *tortillas*, she heaps it in small mounds on the roller. Then she pats each ball out into a large, even circle. One could tell what she is doing by the sounds alone. The noise of her hands

Top: A neighbor grinds the corn on a stone *metate*.
Bottom: Then she heaps *tortilla*-sized mounds of corn on the stone roller.

slapping the dough into shape is loud and slow at first. Then as the corn cake thins and flattens, she pats more lightly, quickly, delicately, and the sound is drier and fainter. As each *tortilla* is finished, she drops it by hand on the hot *comal*, and turns over those that need turning—quickly and lightly, with her fingertips. The *tortillas* dry and brown quickly. Gradually the old woman fills the cloth-lined *canasta*—basket—with soft, fresh *tortillas*—warm, smelling of roasted corn, and ready to be eaten for breakfast.

At last, after several hours of chores, the Hernandez family gathers in the *cocina* around eight o'clock for their breakfast of *café* and fresh *tortillas*. After eating, Arnoldo and Evelia wash their hands, gather up their notebooks, and hurry down to the *plazuela*, calling back, "*Adiós, Mama. Adiós, Papa.*"

Trabajo de las mujeres—
Women's Work

As soon as the dishes from breakfast are washed, Flora and Marylena start on their main work of the day, their cloth business. Like many Indians throughout Latin America, the Hernandezes support themselves by growing much of their own food, by selling some crops, and by practicing a handcraft, such as weaving. In San Antonio the tradition of weaving cloth to sell is an old one that has developed because of the interest of outsiders in the fine handwoven clothing that the women of this village wear.

In Guatemala each woman wears the dress of her village. One can tell at a glance where she comes from, whether one sees her in Antigua or in the capital, Guatemala City, or walking along a country road. Patterns vary from place to place, but the basic designs are similar. The *huipil*—blouse—is always made of two long handwoven rectangles of cloth, which are sewn together, leaving an opening in the center for the head and one at each side for the arms. Some women, near the hot coastal areas, weave short, cool, thin *huipiles*, while others in the cold mountain areas make long, heavy wool and cotton ones that may come down below their knees.

The handwoven *huipil* that San Antonio women wear

Centuries ago the Spanish conquerors were surprised and delighted to see that many Indians made these beautiful textiles. They forced the Indian women to weave cloth that they, the Spanish, could sell in Spain for a great deal of money. Today many people buy Indian cloth—well-off Guatemalans from the city, as well as tourists and exporters from other Latin American countries, from Europe, and from the United States. The cloth of San Antonio is especially prized for its beautiful brocaded designs. This has meant that San Antonio women have a way of earning money and a sense of pride in their traditional Indian skill. It has also meant that the people of San Antonio can continue to live a life of their own.

Several days a week Flora and Marylena go to Antigua to sell pieces of handwoven cloth and the purses that Hipolitó makes on his treadle sewing machine. Since tourists always buy more than the Hernandezes can possibly weave, Flora and Marylena also sell cloth that some of their neighbors have made.

On other days Flora and Marylena work on their own weaving. Here Flora prepares the thread for a new piece. First she drops a loose hank of cotton onto this frame, called a swift, which pivots freely in a circle. She takes the end of the thread, and sitting comfortably, talking with Marylena, begins to wind up a ball, since the thread will be easier to handle this way.

Next Marylena winds thread around dowels set into a heavy piece of wood, the warping frame. These form the lengthwise strands of the finished cloth, and are called the warp. This thread is no

Top: Flora winds up a loose hank of thread into a ball.
Bottom: Marylena winds thread onto the warping frame.

stronger than ordinary sewing cotton, and no threads can be torn, tangled, or crossed, or the weaving will be flawed. Marylena works swiftly and easily at this, never making a mistake. She has been doing it since she was a child, and her body falls into an even rhythm of stretching, bending, turning, stretching, bending, turning, until there are enough threads in place for the desired piece.

Then Flora checks the threads, for the designs are complicated and precise; there must be exactly the right number of threads for each pattern. Here Marylena is setting up her loom, while Flora helps her straighten the warp. The threads have been carefully slipped off the warping frame, and in place of each dowel, a stick is inserted to make the loom. Marylena has looped a long string under every other warp thread and over the stick, which is called a heddle. When she raises the heddle, the alternate warp threads are all lifted

Top: Flora checks the threads for the loom.
Bottom: Marylena begins to weave.

at the same time, and she can weave a row by passing a shuttle full of yarn between the raised threads and the lower ones. One end of the loom is tied to an upright post and the other to Marylena. She tightens and loosens the threads by leaning backward and forward.

This is an ancient kind of loom, used in many parts of the world. Weaving is slow this way, but very complicated patterns can be woven, and the loom has the advantage of being completely portable. If Marylena wants to stop her work or take it somewhere else, she simply steps out of the strap that goes around her hips and rolls the whole loom up into a small bundle.

Marylena began to weave when she was very young, as did all the Indian women in San Antonio. It is as expected that a little girl will learn to weave well, with the help of her mother, aunt, or sister, as that she will learn to brush her hair or dress herself. Even Evelia has her own small loom and has practiced regularly since she was three years old. Flora mentions with curiosity and surprise the one woman in San Antonio who doesn't weave. "She doesn't do women's work. She likes to work with her husband on the farm!"

Maximina and Marta Lopez, who live next door to the Hernandez family, are expert weavers and make some of the cloth that Flora and Marylena sell in Antigua. The Hernandezes supply the thread and pay the Lopezes for the finished cloth. This source of cash is especially important to the Lopez sisters, since their father, David, doesn't own any farmland on which to raise food for the family. Marylena, dropping off some thread, stays

to watch the women weave in their sunny compound. Maximina is working on a heavily brocaded piece of cloth, using a small polished stick, carved by her father, to pick up the warp threads so that she can weave in one of the many bright yarns that form the pattern. This is very slow, very careful work; it will be a long time before the weaving is finished.

Maximina and Marta are pleased with the new supplies that the Hernandezes have bought in Guatemala City. There are many hanks of machine-spun thread in all the brilliant colors they admire. In earlier times Guatemalan Indian women spun their own thread from native-grown cotton and colored it with natural dyes. They made black dye from carbon, and a rich yellow from hydrous iron oxide. Leaves and stalks of certain trees and plants, as well as wild tomatoes, blackberries, and avocados were used for coloring. The women knew how to set the dyes, first

Top and bottom: As Marylena watches, Maximina sets up threads on the backstrap loom and brocades a pattern into her weaving.

with urine, and later with alum, so that they would not fade, run into each other, or wash out altogether. Flora says, "My grandmother knew how to make a red dye from little insects which she gathered in thousands, but I myself have never done this; I don't know how." In all of Guatemala, almost the only naturally colored threads still in use are those made from a cotton boll which is itself a light brown when it grows, not white as is most cotton, and those colored with a deep blackish blue dye made from the indigo plant.

Over the centuries the weavers of San Antonio have slowly incorporated new ideas and influences; the women weave their lives and their history into their cloth. Some of the patterns found on San Antonio *huipiles* today can be seen carved in stone on ancient Mayan monuments. These seemingly abstract designs are really simplified pictures of things found in the Indian world, natural and man-made. A many-colored band is called *arco*—rainbow—and a row of diamond shapes are *pepitas*—seeds. The brilliantly colored fruits, flowers, and animals found on many *huipiles* today are due to the influence of a group of European nuns. More than a hundred years ago they came to San Antonio, to live in the convent next to the church, and taught the Indian women European traditions in weaving and embroidery. The nuns, like the Mayan stone carvers, are long gone, but their designs, as well as the Mayan patterns, are still used. Today the practice of incorporating new ideas continues; small brocaded bicyclists sometimes appear on San Antonio *tsutes!*

Top: All San Antonio women wear belts like this one. *Bottom:* This *huipil* combines Mayan and Spanish patterns.

Trabajo de los hombres—
Men's Work

Among the Indians of Latin America, the work of men is usually quite different from that of women. Women cook the food, clean the home, wash the clothes, look after the children, sell particular crops or goods in the nearest market, and often work at certain crafts. Men farm, practice other crafts, and sell other produce.

David Lopez, Maximina and Marta's father, works at several crafts to support himself and his family. In the dry season he makes adobe bricks from clayey earth found in deposits near San Antonio, and sells them to people who are building new houses or additional rooms in their compounds. At other times he sells *petates*, mats made from the rushes that grow abundantly in the marshy parts of the valley near San Antonio. Soaked in water and flattened, the reeds can easily be woven into springy strong *petates*. Small ones are used by women to sit or kneel on while weaving or cooking; large ones are used for mattresses and house walls.

In the Hernandez household, Hipolitó has learned to operate a sewing machine. From cloth that he buys in Guatemala City, he makes purses that Marylena and Flora sell in Antigua. He says,

Top: David Lopez weaves a rush mat.
Bottom: Hipolitó works on a purse.

"I've done well enough to buy a second machine, so I often hire a boy to help me work."

Hipolitó cuts and sews his cloth slowly, with great care, using even the smallest scraps to advantage. He never works impatiently or hurriedly, and he is always pleased to stop and chat with any neighbor who drops in, to rest a minute and smoke a cigarette, and to attend to Flora and the children when they have something to show him. Like many Latin Americans, he values this way of working at home, and doesn't resent interruptions that may slow down his production.

Hipolitó's business helps bring in cash to buy the many things the Hernandezes want to have but cannot make themselves. He has been putting money aside to make the work area into an enclosed room, with stone and stucco walls and a cement floor, which the Hernandezes would prefer to the present arrangement. He has saved enough to buy the rocks for the foundation, and is unloading them here from the truck in which they were brought to San Antonio. The family is pleased at the possibility of this addition to their house, though they know it will be a long time before it is completed.

Hipolitó, like nearly all the men of San Antonio, spends much of his time farming. The Guatemalan highlands have an ideal climate for raising crops. The sun shines nearly every day, and the temperature is in the seventies all year around. Seeds sprout easily in the warm earth, and are nourished by the rains, which fall almost daily from May to October and occasionally during the other months. The growing season is long, and

Hipolitó's business profits help pay for a new room in their house.

several different crops can be grown on the same piece of land in a single year.

But even with a good climate, the highland farmer has a difficult time. Much of his land is steep and poor in quality. The flat land in the valleys between the hills is the easiest to farm, since it is level. It also has the richest earth, since fertile topsoil washes down from the mountains in the heavy rains. But this prized land is largely owned by a few wealthy Guatemalans, the minority of the population, not by the Indians, who must farm the hillsides.

In the lowlands, along the coast of Guatemala, large companies run the plantations producing rubber, sugar cane, and bananas. These companies, many owned by people from the United States, use complicated modern farming methods to produce huge crops. In this part of Guatemala, too, the Indian has a hard time, since he works these lands as a hired hand, earning less than one *quetzal* —one United States dollar—a day and often getting malaria and other diseases common in the steamy jungle climate.

When Hipolitó was a young man, he worked on a coastal plantation. Now that he is better off, he is able to farm for himself. He raises *maíz*— corn—for his family to eat, and *chiles*—hot peppers—to sell in Guatemala City. This is a common pattern among farmers here, who often raise one cash crop that grows well in their area.

Hipolitó begins his pepper farming by scraping the seeds from dried *chiles* he has saved from the previous year, often hiring David Lopez to help with this. Hipolitó plants the seeds in July in the

David Lopez strips the seeds from dried *chiles*.

upper part of the family compound, covering the ground with old *petates* to hold in the moisture and to prevent the occasionally heavy rain from washing the seeds away. When they have sprouted, he waters them carefully when necessary until they are eight inches tall, big enough to be transplanted. Flora inherited some farmland from her father, but this is too far from San Antonio for Hipolitó to use for the *chiles*, which need frequent care. So each year he rents a small plot of land just outside the village for three *quetzales*—three dollars in United States currency.

Hipolitó says, "If the weather in September, October, and November is good, I sell two or three thousand *chiles* in Guatemala City. If it is bad, I may lose the whole crop."

When it is time to plant his *maíz* in May, Hipolitó travels by bus to the land that Flora inherited. She owns fourteen *cuerdas*, but only four are level enough to use, and even those four are on fairly steep hillsides.

The dimensions of a *cuerda* are based on a measurement called the *vara*, which is the distance from the center of the chest to the tips of the fingers of one outstretched arm—about a yard. A *cuerda* is forty *varas* on each side. The four *cuerdas* that Hipolitó plants in *maíz* make up an area somewhat smaller than a football field. This is a common size for a man to farm here and in much of Latin America. Hipolitó must make many trips to this land over the five months that the corn grows, and sometimes the whole family goes along to help weed and harvest. Their yield is nine *quin-*

Top: The sown *chile* seeds are covered with mats.
Bottom: Hipolitó waters the seedlings in his compound.

tales of dried corn kernels. One *quintal*, a hundred pounds, feeds the family for a little less than a month, so they must buy several more *quintales* each year to have enough *maíz* to eat.

This hillside near San Antonio shows many characteristics of highland farming. The fields are small, as well as steep, since they have been passed down from generation to generation, divided among brothers and sisters for hundreds of years. The field in the center of the picture, covered with grass and bushes, is unused now; it is "resting," lying fallow. Since the highland farmer knows little about the use of fertilizer, and has scant extra cash with which to buy it anyway, the nutriments in the thin soil are used up in several years, and the land must be allowed to recover before it can raise a crop again.

Men are clearing the ground on both sides of the fallow field for new planting. The work they can do is limited entirely by the strength of their bodies, and the skill with which they use two simple tools: the *machete*, a big wide-bladed knife, and the *azadón*, a long-handled heavy hoe. They have no machinery, not even oxen or burros, to help them cultivate the land or carry their crops home. The roots of the grass grow deep, and it is a slow, difficult, tiring job to loosen them, break them up, and turn over the soil, so that seeds may be planted. The men cut down the bushes and most of the trees with their *machetes* —they do not use axes or saws—and laboriously chop them up into firewood. They leave a few trees standing, so that the roots will help to hold the earth—but even so, on this steep slope, the

bare topsoil washes downhill, little by little, in the heavy beating rains.

Maíz has been planted in other fields on this hillside. Here Emilio Santos, Hipolitó's uncle, hoes his land, chopping out weeds, working his way carefully around the peanut vines he has planted in between the *maíz*. This interplanting is common where land is scarce and cultivation is by hand. Tomatoes, squash, cucumbers, may all be grown in this way, crowded into a small space.

Emilio Santos is one of the oldest men in San Antonio. He has been working his land in the same way for more than fifty years. He was taught to farm by his father and his grandfather. He learned when he was very young to use religious signs to decide on the best days to plant, and then to weed carefully around the tender

young corn. He learned to pick a few ears after four months to eat fresh and to harvest the rest a month later, when the corn is dry and suitable for grinding into meal.

When Emilio's crops are good, he gives thanks to the Christian god and to his favorite saints, just as his Mayan ancestors made offerings to their gods. When his crops are damaged by erosion, storm, insects, or plant diseases, there is little he can do to save them.

The Guatemalan government has a pilot project in San Antonio to encourage people to use modern farming practices. Engineers show farmers how to cut their land into level terraces, with ditches at the back of each step to catch the rainwater. On steep slopes, the heavy rain flows rapidly downhill, taking the rich topsoil with it, and

undermining the plants, so that they may fall over. This cannot happen on wide flat terraces. Agronomists tell farmers about crop rotation, a system of planting a series of different crops in successive seasons. Different crops take different minerals from the earth, and some, such as the peanut plant, add nourishment to the soil. Crop rotation can thus keep the soil rich for a long period of time. Agronomists also talk to the farmers about plant diseases and insect control through the use of chemicals, and about increasing the crop yield by using new strains of seeds and by adding fertilizers to the soil.

For a number of reasons, San Antonio farmers are slow to accept these ideas. Many of the practices are new and strange to them and differ sharply from the old, time-tested methods they have used and respected for generations. Their lives and the lives of their families depend completely upon the success of their crops, and since they can barely support themselves now, they dare not take risks. In addition, most farmers have so little extra cash that they must feel convinced the crops will show a marked improvement before they will lay out money for treated seeds, insecticides, and fertilizers. Well-off Indians, like Hipolitó, listen cautiously to the government agricultural experts and try out a few of the ideas that seem good to them. If other farmers, like Emilio Santos, see that there are benefits, they may follow suit.

Learning new agricultural methods may help the Indians grow a bit more food, but in the long run, the only major way to improve their stan-

Torrents of rain on these too steep hillsides have ruined the *maíz* crops.

dard of living is to distribute the fertile land more equally. This is a move that the government and the wealthy people have successfully prevented for a long time. Until it happens, the men of San Antonio will continue to walk several miles to their small steep fields, work long hours, and carry their crops, as much as a hundred pounds at a time, on their backs, back down to the village.

Comidas— Meals

Frijoles and *tortillas* form nearly the whole of the Indians' diet in Latin America. To be strong and healthy, people need an adequate amount of food rich in protein, and beans are almost the only such food that Indians can afford. Protein-rich meat, poultry, fish, and eggs are so expensive that they are only occasionally eaten, and never in the amounts that middle class people in the United States are used to. A single chicken or a pound of beef costs a whole day's pay for a laborer such as David Lopez.

When the Hernandezes are ready to cook the *pollo* they have bought for the christening feast, they ask a neighbor, Francisca Gomez, to come and kill it, since Marylena and Flora do not like to do this. Francisca deftly wrings the chicken's neck and holds it until it stops struggling. Flora helps her to pluck it, and then Francisca moves it around over the fire to singe off the small pinfeathers. She next holds it upside down for a few minutes to let the blood drain into the head, so that she will be able to cut it up neatly. Using fresh water from the *pila*, she carefully washes all the parts to be used, and puts them in a pot of salted water heating over the fire. While the

Flora and her neighbor Francisca prepare a chicken for a christening feast.

pollo is cooking, she grinds *tomates* and *cebollas* —onions—up together, and Flora adds the mixture to the pot. The fire burns brightly, the stew begins to bubble, and delicious smells fill the *cocina*. Francisca and Flora wash the *metate* and roller, the knife, even the table, scrubbing them thoroughly with pads made from dried cornhusks. The water runs off onto the earth and is quickly absorbed.

But a chicken stew like this is a rarity: on most days the Hernandezes do not eat meat, fish, or poultry at all. Day after day their main meal at noon is the same.

In the morning Flora sets a large pot of *frijoles negros*, which have soaked in water overnight, to cook slowly on the tripod over the *cocina* fire.

For flavor she cuts up a *cebolla* or two and adds it to the pot. Sometimes, after the *frijoles* are soft, she sets them aside and cooks a pot of *arroz*—rice —over the tripod. Meanwhile Marylena mashes the *frijoles* through a food mill. Flora makes fresh *tortillas* each noontime, wrapping them up in a clean napkin until the family is ready to eat them.

When Arnoldo and Evelia come home from school, they are given money to buy a piece of *queso*—cheese—from the nearby *tienda*. Evelia usually helps to set the table for lunch. Here she has put out *gaseosas*—soft drinks—which are a special treat. If Miguel, the boy who helps Hipolitó, has been working in the compound, he eats with them, and sometimes a neighbor who has been helping the family does also. Plates are heaped with rich-tasting *frijoles* and *arroz*, and the big *canasta* of *tortillas* is passed around and around

the table. This is a sociable meal, and lasts a long time, with much laughing and exchange of news.

Hipolitó has just come back from the *carpinteria*—carpenter's shop—where he went to buy a chair to replace an old one broken beyond repair. The carpenter was building a wooden coffin, and Hipolitó learned that a neighbor had died in his sleep last night. Each person at the table crosses himself, and then Flora remarks that he was, after all, a very old man, and had been ill for a long time. "*Sí, es verdad, sí.*" Hipolitó answers. "Yes, it's true, yes."

Marylena, smiling, says that her friend, the young Indian teacher in the *colegio parroquial*—Catholic school—in San Antonio, has sent word that he will visit her when the afternoon session of school is over. Miguel and Arnoldo nudge each other under the table and giggle behind their hands. Marylena tells them sternly to be quiet. They grin at each other.

Flora, spreading *frijoles* and *queso* on a *tortilla*, looks at Marylena and smiles. She thinks of herself at Marylena's age, remembering the way she and Hipolitó were then. When Hipolitó went to her mother, to ask to marry Flora, he was put off. Her mother wanted Flora's help at home to cook and clean for the many sons in the family who did not yet have wives. Finally, following a local custom, Flora and Hipolitó ran off together. Then, as they knew she would, the mother went to the *alcalde*—mayor—saying that in view of this scandalous happening the couple must be married at once. So they were married, and Flora

began to live permanently in Hipolitŏ's house with his family, as was the custom. Later Hipolitŏ's mother died, and Hipolitŏ's father divided up the family land in San Antonio. The Hernandezes' present home is on Hipolitŏ's share, and his old father lives next door with Hipolitŏ's brother.

Flora's and Hipolitŏ's marriage has proven to be a good one. They have worked hard and prospered. They enjoy each other, and they agree on important questions in their lives. Hipolitŏ does not drink too much, as some of the men in San Antonio do. None of their children have died, and Flora thanks God for this, for all her life she has seen funeral processions moving through town, with men bearing tiny coffins, heading out to the cemetery.

For the Hernandezes, lunch of beans, rice, *tortillas,* and cheese is a long sociable meal. The soft drinks are an unusual treat.

Flora looks around the table with much satis-faction, for she knows what hardship is from her own experience as well as from her neighbors'. She can still remember her father's death when she was seven. She remembers much hard work. In those days, there were few public buses, and the family walked five hours to their distant farm-land, tending the *maíz*, sleeping in the field, and walking five hours back after the next day's work. She remembers the times when all she had to eat were *tortillas* with salt and *chiles*. She knows that many Indians still live that way. She is very thank-ful that her family is healthy, has good food to eat, and is prosperous enough to send Arnoldo and Evelia to school, instead of keeping them at home to help with the work as many Indians must.

Flora feels that she herself was useless in school, preferring to play instead of study. She says about her own inability to read or write, "*Me gusta, pero ya no puedo.*" "I want to, but I still can't."

She and Hipolitó feel that schooling will help their children deal with the *ladino* world, where written accounts, bills, and regulations often con-fuse or deceive nonliterate Indians.

When the last *tortilla* has been spread with the last bit of *queso* and *frijoles*, when the pot of *arroz* is empty, and Flora has finished up Evelia's *gaseosa*, the meal is over. Marylena washes the dishes with a cornhusk pad, and Flora dries them and puts them back in the screened cupboard.

Meanwhile Evelia and Arnoldo wash their faces and hands, smooth back their hair, and hurry down to the *plazuela* for the afternoon ses-sion of school.

Marylena scrubs the dishes with a cornhusk pad.

Escuela—
School

As Arnoldo and Evelia near the *plazuela*, they can hear the shouts of the children playing and the slap-slap of bare feet running across the hard-packed ground. When the bell rings, the last children finish brushing their teeth at the *pila* and run to line up in front of the *escuela nacional*—national or public school. Evelia rushes past the *iglesia*—church—to her school, which is in the old convent. Arnoldo takes his place in front of the *escuela nacional* with the boys of his class. When all the children are standing in neat lines, they are permitted to file into the stone building. The central hall is dark and cool, and even the smallest sound bounces loudly off the hard walls and floor. Arnoldo's classroom is the last one on the left, and as he and his classmates enter the room, they are greeted by the *profesora*—teacher. She is a young *ladino* woman who lives in Antigua and takes the bus each day to San Antonio. For working in this crowded and noisy building, she has a perfect voice—one that cuts through the din without adding to it.

As soon as Arnoldo and his classmates are seated, the *profesora* begins putting some math problems on the blackboard. It is hard for the

Feet crossed, a girl studies a math problem.

children to see the board. The room is lit by sunlight coming in the side windows, and the light strikes the blackboard, causing a glare. There are two bare electric-light bulbs hanging from the ceiling, but they are not turned on. The *profesora* chooses one of the girls to work at the board, and Arnoldo and the rest of the class take out their notebooks and copy the problem: 98) 567.853678031. Writing 5 on the board, the girl works aloud, "*Cinco por ocho . . . ,*" "Five times eight . . . ," while the students in their seats set to work on the same problem. When everyone has finished, the *profesora* walks around, correcting each notebook. Then she returns to the board, erases the finished problem, and writes a new one. Another student is chosen to work at the blackboard; everyone else writes this problem in his or her notebook, and the process starts all over again. There are no textbooks. The arithmetic lesson lasts nearly an hour. The students become restless and have a hard time paying attention. Some girls take out their embroidery. Arnoldo listens to the voices from the girls' first-grade class next door.

They are having a phonics lesson. Arnoldo knows the *profesora* is pointing to a picture of a pineapple when the girls all scream "*piña,*" and to a picture of a young girl when they scream "*niña.*" He can almost see the room, with the little girls crammed together at long desk-tables and the walls covered with reading charts. After a while he hears the *profesora* say, "*Bien, clase; ahora,* Yolanda." "Fine, class; now, Yolanda." He can hear Yolanda's thin voice plainly as she recites

Top: Arnoldo copies a math problem into his notebook.
Bottom: First-grade girls strain to see the pictures.

the list alone: "*Piña . . . niña . . . mañana . . . dueño.*" "Pineapple . . . girl . . . tomorrow . . . owner." The *profesora* says, "*Muy bien,* Yolanda"—"Very fine, Yolanda"—and the little girls applaud energetically.

The girls in this class range in age from four to seven. It is their first year in school, since the *escuela nacional* does not have a kindergarten. The girls, like most other San Antonio children, come to school barefoot and have so little money that pencils must be shared by breaking them into three pieces. While the school itself is free, the parents must provide their children with pencils and notebooks, and for many of them this expense is a hardship. It is an even greater hardship to have a child in school when that child might be helping the parents in their work or even earning money by working for others. Parents endure these hardships because they believe that school is important for their children. They know the children must learn to speak Spanish to succeed in the *ladino* world. Hopefully, they will learn to read and write it too and also learn some basic arithmetic. In addition, the parents are glad to have their children get the free milk and bread that is served daily to some classes. Most parents can afford to send their children to school for only a few years, so after the third grade, as the working or earning ability of the child grows, enrollment drops, especially among the girls. Parents don't seem to think schooling is as important for girls as for boys. Of the thirty students in the sixth grade, only seven are girls. There are only thirteen girls in Arnoldo's class of thirty-seven.

Much of the curriculum, copied from schools in Europe, is out of place in San Antonio. Instead of learning about their own rich Mayan history, the children memorize facts about Robespierre and Marie Antoinette. They must memorize far more complex math and history and geography than children in the same grade in the United States. In reality, their education consists almost totally of memorizing information that would prepare them for high school. San Antonio, however, does not have a high school, and few, if any, Indian parents can afford to send their children to high school in Antigua.

The schools are beginning to change, and to try to make their courses more useful to the students. The *escuela nacional*, for example, has had great success in introducing the children to proper

Some children study; others play or daydream.

dental care. Each classroom has a rack with cups and toothbrushes and a supply of toothpaste. All students are required to brush their teeth daily at school. The Catholic school in San Antonio—*colegio parroquial*—has begun instruction in woodworking, agriculture, and sewing.

The *colegio parroquial*, Evelia's school, is different in many ways from the *escuela nacional*. It is located on the other side of the *plazuela*, next to the *iglesia* and across from the *puesto de salud* —health clinic. The building is very old, and was once the church convent that housed the nuns who brought the European designs to San Antonio weavers. The school is small, consisting of three classrooms located around a tiny inner courtyard. Here the bright sunlight streams down on a *pila*, and birds fly in and out among the trees. One of the classes is held in the covered open hallway. The teachers here are Indian and

Trees frame this hallway classroom.

speak the native language of San Antonio—Cakchiquel—although they teach their classes in Spanish, so that the children will learn it. The principals—a couple who run the school together—live in San Antonio. The classes are smaller here than at the *escuela nacional,* and the parents must pay to have their children attend. Flora and Hipolitó pay one and a half *quetzales* a month for Evelia to go to first grade, and they are pleased to be able to afford this. Second grade will cost two *quetzales* a month, third grade, two and a half *quetzales,* and so on.

The parents of the students at the *colegio parroquial* take great interest in the program of instruction. Flora says she wants to make sure that no time is wasted and that Evelia will learn useful skills. Flora and Hipolitó speak quite differently about the *escuela nacional.* Because it is run by the government, the parents do not dare to question the program. They know the government is powerful, and they must accept what it does, not tell it what they want it to do.

In Evelia's class, each child has his or her own desk. Here the *profesora,* Magdalena Chicol, puts some first-grade arithmetic problems on the board. As the students copy the work in their notebooks, Señorita Chicol goes on to help the second graders with a multiplication problem: "*Quatro por ocho, trienta y dos.*" "Four times eight, thirty-two." While the children work, the teacher walks around, helping those who are stuck, encouraging and praising others. Then, when the problems are done, Evelia and the other students bring their books to her desk to be corrected. Evelia's is

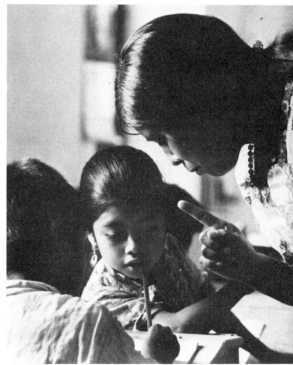

Top: A math lesson in Evelia's classroom
Bottom: The *profesora* speaks to a boy behind Evelia.

marked MB for *muy bueno*—very good. After arithmetic, the next lesson begins with Evelia reading aloud: "*En la escuela los niños aprenden a leer. Ellos escriben cuentas y muchas cosas útiles y interesantes.*" "In school, the children learn to read. They write stories and many useful and interesting things." Then the book is passed to the next student, Cristina, who takes her turn at reading aloud. When the story is finished, Señorita Chicol asks questions. "*Qué me pueden decir?*" "What can you tell me?" and everyone answers at once: "*Los niños aprenden a leer.*" "The children learn to read." "*Los niños aprenden a escribir.*" "The children learn to write." "*Los niños escriben cuentos.*" "The children write stories."

After reading, it is time for a break, and the whole school lines up by class and walks out to the

playing field to practice marching. Soon they will be in a parade celebrating the independence of Guatemala from Spain. Evelia is very excited and is looking forward to the big day. She will have a new *falda* to wear, and also a fine new *cinturón*.

While she is marching, she dreams of her new *falda* and has a hard time remembering which foot is which. Señorita Chicol is always nearby, gently helping her and the other young students. When the practice is over, the drummer leads the children back to the school for the last class of the day.

Evelia and the *niñas* in her room are learning to embroider—flowers, birds, letters, and phrases—on pieces of white cloth. The boys work designs on pieces of burlap. The first graders are tired from their six hours in school. The day is warm and still, and flies buzz monotonously around the room. The children listen to the flies drone, and to the sounds from the other rooms.

Next door the children in a woodworking class are cutting out shelves. Their teacher, a young Indian who has always lived in San Antonio, shows them how to use simple handtools—saws and drills and planes.

Outside, in the hallway classroom, José Luis Cuxil talks with his pupils about agriculture. He explains that terracing and the use of fertilizer can protect the land and at the same time increase the production of *maíz*.

After the classroom discussion, Señor Cuxil and some of his students take the bus to the nearby village of Dueñas. There, in the churchyard, Padre Frank has organized a practical course in ag-

Top: Señorita Chicol encourages the children.
Bottom: José Cuxil talks thoughtfully about farming.

riculture. By applying to participate in a government program, he has obtained the services of an agronomist, Jorge Velasquez, who comes to Dueñas twice a week to teach the children.

First the students level the planting surface and carefully remove all the large stones and clods. Then Padre Frank and Señor Velasquez help them lay out the planting lines with string. Señor Velasquez instructs in the placing of seeds—two in each hole. "In case the first doesn't go, then the second will," he tells them.

Everyone sets to planting. Some use sticks to make the seed holes and to measure the distance between them. Others find that fingers work just as well. While the boys are planting, Señor Velasquez and Señor Cuxil instruct the girls. Their job is to cover the seeds with earth and put leaves

Top: Padre Frank helps level the planting area.
Bottom: With a finger a boy pokes holes for seeds.

over the earth to protect the seeds while they are germinating. The girls giggle a little, perhaps feeling awkward as they take part in what has always been considered men's work.

Padre Frank watches the children at work, and he is pleased. With this class his hopes for the villagers are starting to be realized. He wants education to be useful to the people—to help them survive in the modern world—and at the same time preserve their own values and ways. He says, "There should be enough activities for youth in the towns to make a good life here without wanting to go to the city and wait in line for something that never comes.

"I would like to start an institution for boys where they can learn things they enjoy that are useful to them—farming, carpentry, electricity, mechanics, plumbing—but I wouldn't be satisfied with just plumbing. I want to add some culture. There should be programs of language—poetry, drama, writing—so the Indians will be respected and not get fooled."

He realizes that the Indian life-style must develop and grow. He says, "I want to help them be ready for the flood of civilization that will come in the next five or ten years. They must have a briefing on the technological world, so nothing comes as a miracle that would call upon their awe."

The students are pleased with the class, too: They talk eagerly to each other about it as they ride back in the bus to San Antonio. Some of their fathers attend a course that Señor Velasquez gives at night. Often the children read aloud

Top: Señor Velasquez gives directions to the girls.
Bottom: A group of girls cover the seeds.

the mimeographed manual for this course to their parents and talk with them about old and new methods of farming.

By the time the students reach San Antonio, it is four o'clock, and both schools are letting out for the day. Some children go directly home to help their families with chores, but many stop to play awhile in the *plazuela*.

Small groups of *niñas* seek out quiet places for a game of jacks; this is a favorite of Evelia's, and she is already quite skillful. Arnoldo likes to try throwing the *trompo*—top—with his friends. He is pleased when he is able to land it in a steady spin on the ground and then slide his hand carefully under it without stopping its motion. He laughs at the tickle of its base on his palm and also with pleasure at his success.

Top: Evelia and her friends play jacks.
Bottom: Arnoldo throws his *trompo*.

The large open center of the *plazuela* makes a perfect place for playing soccer, and almost immediately a game starts, the teams growing in size as more boys join. Throughout Latin America, soccer is a favorite sport, and San Antonio is no exception.

Some girls play tag in front of the church, and others climb up on its facade. From here they have a fine view of the whole *plazuela* and can see what's happening at the *escuela nacional*, at the central *pila*, in the cloth-selling stalls, at the *juzgado*—mayor's office—and the jail.

In San Antonio, the only large-scale piece of play equipment is a swing set. The children use the few toys they have or can make—and when they tire of them, they watch the village activities, much as children in the United States watch television after school. The *plazuela* is the center of San Antonio life, and here the children learn about the community.

Puesto de salud—
Health Clinic

These three girls have stopped their games to watch the unloading of medical supplies at the *puesto de salud*—health clinic—near the *plazuela*. A car in San Antonio is unusual enough to be worth watching; no one in San Antonio owns one. This station wagon comes regularly now, and is almost as well known as Padre Frank's jeep.

San Antonio is unusual in having a clinic; many communities in Latin America do not. Many Indians never see a doctor or a nurse in their whole lives. For some sicknesses and other health problems, traditional Indian methods of curing are effective; for others, modern medical care is needed. So one morning a week people wait patiently at the clinic to see the government doctor, who shares his services among a number of villages. And every afternoon they line up to see Alicia Cajia, the *enfermera*—nurse—who works here full time.

Señorita Cajia is only nineteen; yet she treats with energy and intelligence as many of the five thousand people of San Antonio as come to see her. She works constantly to overcome their well-founded distrust of *ladinos*, and she talks nonstop about sanitation, inoculations, good nutrition, while she is treating people.

Medical supplies are brought to the new health clinic.

Here she is preparing to vaccinate a little boy against whooping cough. She raises her voice over the protesting yells of the child, and explains to the mother that even though the shot hurts, the medicine she is putting into his body is good, and it will prevent him from ever getting whooping cough. She says that she wants to vaccinate all the children in San Antonio against whooping cough and also against smallpox and measles. She has enough medicine now to do it, and she urges the mother to tell her neighbors to bring their children to the clinic. The mother nods, saying, "*Gracias, señorita,*" as she leaves.

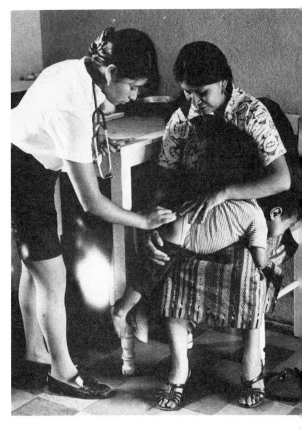

The next woman says her baby has diarrhea, and no matter what herbal medicines or different foods she gives him, it doesn't stop. He is still nursing, but now that he is nearly two years old he also eats the same food as the rest of the family. Last week his older sister had the sickness, and before that, his grandmother. The mother talks as best she can in Spanish so that she will be understood, since Señorita Cajia does not know Cakchiquel. The mother has brought a small clean bottle to the clinic, and she listens while Señorita Cajia explains why she cannot fill it with medicine.

"I'm sorry, I have nothing I can give your baby. That medicine always runs out quickly. But there are things you can do at home to help keep your children healthy. It is important to cover all your food, so that flies cannot get on it. Flies carry the sickness your baby has, from one person to another. It is important to wash your hands when you prepare food, and to instruct your children to wash theirs before they eat. It is important to

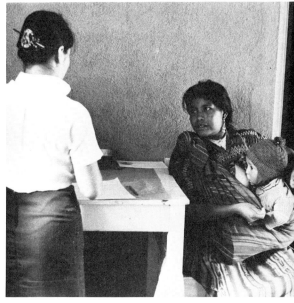

A baby, vaccinated against whooping cough by Señorita Cajia, nurses for comfort.

keep your dishes and pots clean. Do not let your baby pick things up from the ground and put them in his mouth. You should give him a bath every day."

Señorita Cajia speaks very rapid Spanish, and she talks very loudly, as though that will make her words more understandable. Her voice when loud is rather shrill and seems to fill the whole room. The mother struggles to understand, for she has heard from her neighbors that some of these medicines are good; but many of the *enfermera*'s words go by too quickly for her to grasp.

Now an old man comes in for his eighth rabies shot. He was bitten by a rabid dog, which later died, and now he must have fourteen shots, one each day. The treatment is very painful, but it is essential; if rabies develops, the patient nearly always dies. Señorita Cajia explains to him, as she has each time, that people must avoid any animal that is foaming at the mouth, trying to attack people, or otherwise behaving strangely. The old man understands very little Spanish, but he can pick up more of what the *enfermera* says now than he could seven days ago. In the past week he has come to like and trust her, for he sees that she is working hard to help people.

The old man, like many people in San Antonio, is learning that Señorita Cajia is very different from most *ladino* medical people that Indians have seen and heard about all their lives. In the old days, when there were no buses between San Antonio and Antigua, it was very difficult to get medical care. A sick person was tied in a chair, and then a strong man put a tumpline around the chair and carried it on his back all the way to Antigua. Once there the troubles were far from over. The small hospital was crowded, and private *ladino* doctors were expensive and unfriendly. Today it is far easier to get to Antigua, but the Indians still have problems with *ladino* doctors and the Spanish language. Padre Frank, who feels keenly that Indians are often treated badly by the *ladino* world, tells it this way.

"The Indian goes to the doctor and says—trying to speak in Spanish so that the doctor will understand him—'I was sick.'

"The doctor says, 'You *were* sick? So you're well now?'

"The Indian is confused, because he thinks that he said, 'I am sick.' To him the tense makes no difference. I *was* sick or I *am* sick or I *will* be sick —it's all sick.

"The doctor says, 'You were sick. What did you have?'

" 'I don't know.'

" 'Well,' the doctor asks, 'You're over it now?'

"The Indian thinks, what's the use of getting into a big argument over something I don't understand. Besides, the doctor must know; he is a doctor. So the Indian says, 'Yes, I am not sick now.'

" 'Well,' the doctor answers, 'Then what did you come here for?' "

The Guatemalan government is trying in a small way to improve medical care for the Indians. Señorita Cajia trained at a nursing school in the capital for two years at government expense. In return for this free education, she has agreed to work for two years in any village where she is needed. She feels that her job in San Antonio is often hard and lonely. She says of her meager supplies, "*Hay poco. Ni tanto equipo, ni medicinas. Muy poquito.*" "There is very little. Neither enough equipment nor medicine. Very, very little." In spite of the hardships she enjoys her work. "I like to be where I am needed," she says.

An important link between the villagers and the world of *ladino* medicine is the voluntary, unpaid committee of San Antonio men who maintain the clinic and distribute a free food supplement. Señorita Cajia knows that malnutrition is the main problem in San Antonio, that people often have great difficulty withstanding mild infections, as well as serious diseases, simply because they are not adequately nourished. When she sees people with malnutrition, she tells the committee members to give them two cups a week of the diet supplement stored in the clinic; she wishes she could give them more, but there is not enough.

Here a member of the committee is giving a supply of the supplement to one of the girls for her sick brother. The girl has known this man all her life, so she is neither afraid nor shy. She listens while he explains in Cakchiquel that the powder is made of cornmeal, dried milk, and soybean flour, and that it can be mixed with water, hot or cold, and used either as a drink or in cooking. He says, "It is good, it will help make your brother strong. Now take it home to your mother."

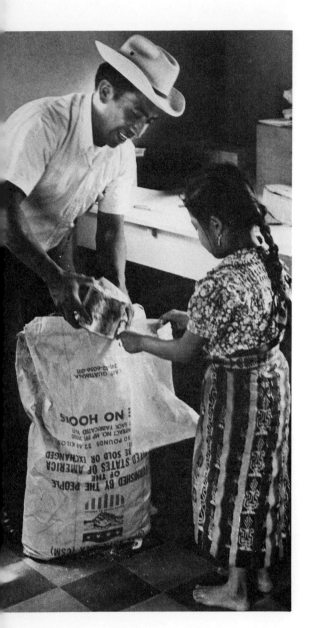

Free food supplement is given for a sick boy.

Gobierno—
Government

Next door to the *puesto de salud* is the *juzgado*—office of the *alcalde*—mayor—the courthouse and seat of local government. The *alcalde* is helped by a *ministril*, whose job is to keep order in the town. While many of his duties are like a policeman's, the *ministril* does not wear a uniform or carry a gun.

The *ministriles* are appointed by the *alcalde* and his council, and each serves for one week, several times a year. It is quite common to hear a man say, "No, I'm not in my fields, I'm in my week now." This means that he is spending that particular week giving service to the village, rather than farming. Having many people take turns as *ministril* gives lots of men the responsibility of handling village affairs, and this seems to lead to a real understanding of the problems. Most families make a great effort to obey the rules and cooperate with each other. The villagers are very proud of their community and want to give service to it. It is a man's government, however, and women are not asked to hold office. In this, the government is much like the family, where it is the man who makes decisions and is in control.

People send for the *ministril* when someone is

drunk or needs help, and on the rare occasions when there is a fight. On this particular day two men have been brought to the *juzgado* to settle an argument. Earlier a woman came running into the *plazuela*, calling out that there was trouble. The *ministril* grabbed up his stick and started off at a run, following the woman to a compound at the edge of San Antonio. Two angry men were arguing, yelling and gesturing, and hitting at each other. The *ministril*, who knew them both, also knew that this was the same argument they had been having on and off for several months. He decided to take them to the *alcalde* to settle it. The *ministril* and a helpful neighbor escorted the men, still arguing, to the *juzgado*.

When they reached the porch of the building, the *ministril* stepped aside to speak to the *auxiliar* —mayor's assistant—whose job it is to enter the chambers of the *alcalde*, report to him, and find out if he can see the people who have come. A person does not have the right to go in to see the *alcalde* without first getting permission from the *auxiliar*. Hipolitó is proud to have served as *auxiliar*. He was appointed by the *alcalde* and gave his service two years ago.

After a few minutes the present *auxiliar* reports that the *alcalde* will see the men, and they enter the *juzgado*. The doors close, and when their feet touch the cool tile floor, the men become quiet for the first time. They walk slowly across the bare courtroom, and stand in front of the *alcalde*, Juan Bautista Lopez Martinez. On the wall behind him hang the staves—symbols of office belonging to the *alcalde* and council. Above the staves is a painting

of the *quetzal*, the bird that is the symbol of Guatemala and the central government. The men know and like the *alcalde*. They voted for him in the recent election, and they feel he is a good man, one whom they can trust.

Señor Martinez greets each of the men by name, inquires after members of their families, and begins to ask questions about their dispute. He speaks carefully and with dignity as he tries to understand the difficulty. Finally he offers a solution—a compromise—in which each man gains a little and gives up a little.

The men feel that they have been well treated and that their problems have been given serious attention. Each is satisfied with the compromise, and they agree to the plan. The *alcalde* is also pleased. He has been able to suggest a good solution because he knows the men and the situation

Señor Martinez listens to the problems of the men.

very well. He also knows that they will abide by the compromise.

Señor Martinez next sentences a man, Alberto Rodriguez, to five days in jail for causing a great disturbance while he was drunk the night before. Señor Rodriguez could have paid a fine of two and a half *quetzales*, or fifty *centavos* for each day of his sentence instead of going to jail, but he did not have the money. He could also have worked off the fine in service to the town, but he has accepted the jail term instead. If Señor Rodriguez's offense had been more serious and his fine more than five *quetzales*, his case would have been taken to Antigua for settlement.

The *ministril* and Señor Rodriguez's wife escort him to his cell next door to the *juzgado;* then his wife goes home to get supplies. Señor Rodriguez is disappointed that the other cell is empty; he had hoped to have someone to talk to. His cell has an earthen floor and three stone walls. The fourth wall, made of bars, faces on the *plazuela*, and he stands there watching the activity. Soon his wife returns with his sister and her son, bringing a *petate* and a blanket for his bed, a *canasta* of hot *tortillas*, and a small pot of *frijoles* for his dinner, and a sweater for the cool night. After she has handed these things through the bars and promised to return in the morning with breakfast *café*, she leaves.

As Señor Rodriguez finishes his dinner, he waves to a friend who is walking by the *pila*. The friend comes over, and they share a cigarette and talk for a while. Señor Rodriguez's five-day sentence will continue to be carried out in this way.

A prisoner talks with his wife and family.

Each day his wife will come with food and clean clothes, and every now and then a friend will stop and talk. The rest of the time he will sleep or watch the people in the *plazuela.*

Another of the duties the *alcalde* has is to make rules for specific events. For instance, when the creek on the edge of town overflowed last year the *alcalde* decreed that every man come and give two hours of work to reinforce the banks. This decree was carried by the *ministril,* who went from place to place in the village, beating a drum and calling out the news to the people.

Señor Martinez does more than just take care of the day-to-day affairs of the village. He says, "It is my job to search after the town's needs. For example, in spite of everyone's efforts, our slaughterhouse was damaged in last year's flood. We need a new one for greater animals—cattle—and also for pigs. We have the piece of land for it, and approval from the government has already been given. Soon I will gather the men to build it."

In San Antonio and villages like it, there is another official, a secretary, who has a great deal of power in the local government. He is an outsider, a *ladino* appointed by a court in Guatemala City, and paid a salary. Most secretaries are more interested in the importance of their job than in the welfare of the village they serve. Usually the secretary does not speak the local Indian language, and makes no attempt to learn the names of the people in the community. Most secretaries hope that their job in a small village will make them look good, and that later they will be appointed to a high post in a more important place.

The secretary prepares papers for the *alcalde.*

While in the eyes of the villagers the *alcalde* is the symbol of government, it is the secretary who makes many important decisions. He has connections in the central government and the authority to talk to officials in Antigua and Guatemala City. It is the job of the secretary to collect taxes in San Antonio. Some taxes are sent to the central government; some remain in San Antonio for the needs of the town. It is the secretary, not the *alcalde*, who knows how much money there is and decides how it is to be spent.

In Guatemala, as in many other Latin American countries, power is tightly held in the capital. The *alcalde* can decide on only very small local matters. The people vote only for candidates to be elected to office; they cannot vote on laws or policies. The Indian in a village like San Antonio knows the name of the *presidente* but little more about the central government. He knows it is *ladino*. He knows that the men who run it are educated and powerful. As Padre Frank says, "The Indian thinks he has to be in good standing with the central government because it is a terrible force. He thinks he can do nothing except try not to get hit by the force."

Mercado—

Market

San Antonio is a community of weavers and farmers, with its own *tiendas, escuelas, iglesia, puesto de salud,* and *juzgado.* But it is not a trading center, and it has no market of its own for the exchange of goods. Most of the crops and handcrafts of San Antonio must be taken elsewhere to be sold, and most of the goods San Antonio people buy must be purchased outside the village.

The small city of Antigua buys many of the fruits and vegetables raised in San Antonio, and it also serves as an exchange center for the towns around it. Farm products from distant parts of the country, factory-made goods from Guatemala City, and articles imported from other countries are all brought to Antigua. A large market is held there several times a week and on those days the people of San Antonio pack up their goods and make an early start for the city.

The Hernandezes, in addition to buying things they need in the market and in the town shops, sell their cloth in the *parque central.* Flora remembers that when she was a child, she and her mother and brothers had to walk the five hilly miles to Antigua and back at the end of the long day. She says, "There were no buses. We went on foot." Now there is a large network of public

transportation that is inexpensive enough for almost everyone to use. Before sunup on market day, buses start running back and forth between Antigua and all the surrounding villages in a pattern like a giant spider web.

The early morning bus rattling down the hill into San Antonio can be heard in the Hernandezes' compound. Flora helps her sister-in-law Estrella load one of the heavy baskets filled with cloth onto her head. Flora and Marylena carry the others. Since it is Saturday, the whole family is going to Antigua. They all hurry out to the place where the bus has stopped, load their bundles on the roof, and climb inside. "*Shak,*" they greet their neighbors in Cakchiquel and say, "*Buenos días,*" to the *ladino* driver.

Soon all the seats are filled. Then the driver and his *ayudante*—helper—begin at the back of the bus to put small boards over the aisle, between each pair of adjacent seats. This way there is room for more people to sit, and they continue to crowd in until the bus is packed to bursting. Babies in *tsutes* on their mothers' backs are pulled around in front, so that the mothers can lean against the seats. Children are lifted onto adults' laps, and bundles of fragile, sweet-smelling flowers—roses, daisies, zinnias—are piled on top of the children. People squeeze together as much as they can to make room for their neighbors, and no one complains at the crowding. When the bus is filled inside and piled high on top with sacks of vegetables, rolls of *petates*, and bundles of cloth, the *ayudante* jumps onto the side or the back and calls out the signal to start, "*¡Dele!*"

Flora helps Estrella lift her heavy load.

The bus bounces and jolts along the narrow dirt road out of the valley, past two or three small hamlets, past farm plots and *café* plantations, past a river where women are already washing their clothes and spreading them to dry on the grassy banks. The road winds around the volcano Agua, a tall sweeping cone of deep blue against the paler morning sky. The passengers talk a bit sleepily or doze as the bus rattles on. Babies nurse; children lean their heads against their parents' warm shoulders, waiting patiently for the ride to end.

The bus rattles to a stop near the Antigua *mercado*—market—and the passengers begin to unfold, climb down stiffly, and stretch. They collect their bundles, which the *ayudante* loads onto their heads or backs, and move off toward the *mercado*.

The bus is unloaded at the Antigua market.

The Hernandez family separates now. Mary-lena, Estrella, and the children head for the *parque central* to lay out their cloth for sale to the many tourists who come there. Arnoldo will sit with them until it is time for the Saturday morning movie—Hipolitó has given him the money for it—and he is excited about seeing the Hollywood Western that is being shown this week. Hipolitó and Flora join the crowds converging on the *mercado*, for today they need to buy a *quintal* of *maíz* and several other things. They pass men and women carrying all kinds of bundles—flowers, fruit, vegetables, blankets, pottery, even furniture. The women stand very straight; they hold their heads steady beneath the heavy baskets, and take small quick steps along the uneven way. The men, bent over by burdens that weigh nearly as

much as they do, almost run, looking out for people and other obstacles as best they can.

Most men and women must carry their goods, at least from the bus to the *mercado*. Some people balance huge loads on their heads; others use a tumpline—a leather strap worn across the forehead and secured to a rope which surrounds the load carried on the back. A few people from nearby hamlets use pack animals—burros and horses. Truck drivers, who have come up from the plantations of the hot coastal area, are parked at the market entrance. They load carriers, men who run in and out of the *mercado*, with bunches of green bananas and rounds of coarse brown sugar.

The *mercado* is held inside the walls of an old ruined church and convent that takes up an entire city block. Everyone who comes to sell goods enters through the front gate or the back, pays a small tax, and heads for his or her accustomed place.

Hipolitó and Flora make their way toward the section of the *mercado* where *maíz* is sold. Here all the sellers are farmers with bags of their own dried kernels and middlemen whose business is to sell *maíz* they have bought from the many farmers who don't come to the market themselves. This man is winnowing his corn so that the kernels will be clean and free from bits of husk and cob. Flora and Hipolitó move quietly from seller to seller, examining carefully all the *maíz*— *amarillo*, *blanco*, and *negro*—yellow, white, and black. Is it clean? Are there any insects in it? They feel the smooth dry kernels: Are they large and full? They ask the price of each bag, then move on to the next. When they find *maíz* that

Top: Bananas are loaded on a man's back.
Middle: At the market entrance a woman pays the tax.
Bottom: A seller cleans his corn of husk and cob.

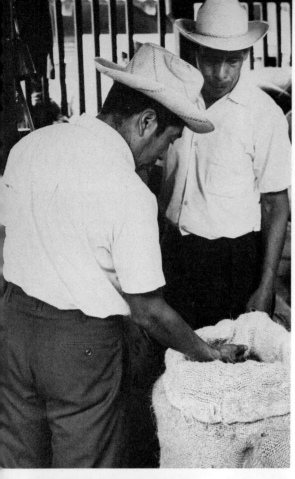

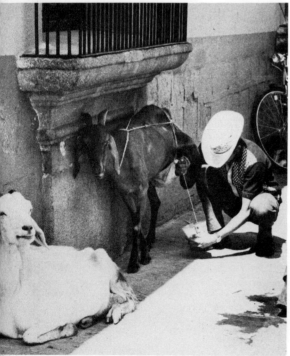

suits them, Hipolitó quietly offers a lower price than what the man is asking, but in an offhand manner, as though he has little interest in this particular sack. The seller refuses, then seemingly casually, suggests a price somewhat lower than his original one. He agrees to Hipolitó's next offer, which is higher than the first one. Hipolitó pays him, and the two men transfer the grain into a burlap bag that Hipolitó has brought with him.

Hipolitó carries the heavy sack out of the *mercado* to a place where he can leave it until the family is ready to return to San Antonio, and Flora goes on to buy some household supplies.

The sun is high now; the *mercado*, sunny and warm. This is the most crowded time, and Flora must move slowly through the people. *Ladino* sellers with armfuls of goods wend their way through the crowds, calling loudly. Their voices rise shrilly above the murmuring tones of the Indians bargaining quietly with each other, above the muffled cheeps of chickens, and the distant sounds of trucks and buses still rumbling along the cobbled streets outside the market.

To those unfamiliar with the *mercado*, it looks like a great haphazard jumble of goods—heaped up in stalls and stands, laid out on the pavement and the ground—so crowded that there is scarcely room for people to pass each other in the narrow open spaces. But beneath this confusion is an order understood by all who use the *mercado*. Nearly everything people need is sold somewhere, and since sellers return to the same places each market day, buyers know where to find them.

Do you want a glass of fresh warm milk? This man milks his goat while you wait. There are many

Top: Hipolitó carefully examines a sack of corn.
Bottom: Fresh goat milk is for sale at the market.

sellers like him who have no stalls at all. In an open space another man spreads out his lumps of *cal*—lime for softening *maíz*. This woman has only one basket of *chuchitos* to sell. She will sit here patiently hour after hour to make a total profit of less than a *quetzal* on the small cornmeal and *tomate* snacks she has cooked at home.

The most substantial stalls are in the dark roofed part of the *mercado* and are equipped with counters, shelves, and electric lights. *Ladinos* run these stalls, and sell mostly manufactured goods—clothing, small hardware, plastic household goods. Here are the straw hats that nearly every man and boy in Guatemala wears. A father and son carefully select what for them is a major

purchase—a new hat for the boy. Is it well made? Will it last a very long time? Can they afford it? Finally one is chosen, and the father quietly bargains the price down to one he knows to be reasonable.

In an open-air section are nearly a dozen stalls where products made of plant fibers are sold. The proprietors of these stalls buy goods from the people who make them, and resell them here. There are pale tan reed baskets of all sizes, string bags dyed brilliant purple, green, and orange, scrub brushes, brooms, rope, and braided halters for horses or burros. Here San Antonio people sell *petates* in all sizes. Nearby a woman unpacks a crate of dried cornhusks which she will sell to *chuchito* makers, who wrap them around the cornmeal before steaming it. This section of the market has a light sweet smell of dried grass like that of a new-mown field or a barn full of fresh hay.

The most fragrant part of the *mercado* is where *flores*—flowers—are sold. Dozens of different kinds of *flores* are grown in the towns and villages around Antigua. The Indians who raise them sell quantities of white daisies, brilliant zinnias, bunches of delicate baby's-breath, spicy carnations, and tall bundles of gladiolus. Many Antigua people buy *flores* every market day, to decorate their rooms and household altars.

Nearby, the smell of food cooking over charcoal fires fills the air. Here the people who have come to the *mercado* for the day can sit at long wooden tables and eat. Some women sell *atole*, a warm fragrant drink made of corn gruel, spiced

A new hat is a big purchase for this boy.

with chocolate or ground *chile* according to the buyer's taste. *Atole* is an early morning favorite, for it fills and warms one quickly. For the main meal of the day some women cook spicy stews and soups of meat-flavored broth and squash. Others fry delicious *chiles rellenos*—peppers which have been stuffed with chopped meat and vegetables. Crisp *tortillas* spread with *frijoles* and *queso* are sold all day long.

People enjoy eating here, for it is a place where they can gather news of conditions and events in many parts of Guatemala. In a country where many people do not read or see television, and some do not listen to the radio, markets serve the function of spreading information. A woman who came to Antigua on an early morning bus describes a road accident she saw along the way. A farmer from the highlands explains that potatoes now cost a lot to buy because the mountain farms produced only a small crop. A bus driver tells about preparations for the big Independence Day parade in the capital.

The *mercado* is also a workshop for artisans. Sandalmakers cut soles for shoes out of old rubber tires and run strips of inner tubing through them for laces. A craftsman cuts, braids, then hammers smooth the strong leather strips for tumplines. An old man mends pots, using metal patches and solder heated on a charcoal brazier. Even a pot with a hole as large as this one is cheaper to mend than to replace, and to the poorest people such savings are important.

Flora has slowly made her way to the section where pottery is sold. Her bean pot has a crack in

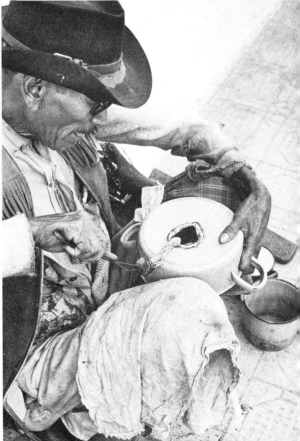

Top: Leather tumplines are made right in the market.
Bottom: A pot with a big hole is still worth mending.

it, and she thinks it may soon break altogether. She sees the rows of pots right away and then pretends to ignore them. She looks at a small mug, picks up a water jar, examines the rows of balance scales hanging overhead. She knows that if she shows too much interest in the pots, the woman running the stall will ask a very high price. On the other hand, the woman realizes that Flora is apt to look at a number of things before asking the price of the one she really wants, and waits quietly until she does so. It is a formal custom they are carrying out.

The seller uses the time to look closely at Flora to see what she can afford to pay. Are her clothes worn or cheap? Not at all. Is she barefoot? No. Are her earrings expensive? Yes, they are. Her belt finely woven? It is. Flora is an Indian, but clearly a prosperous one. Her *huipil* alone tells the seller this, for it is a new one—the velvet at the neck and armholes isn't worn at all—and it is magnificently patterned.

Flora meanwhile begins to check out the bean pots. She picks up one that is smoothly glazed on the inside, for food will soak into any porous unglazed places and the pot will be impossible to clean thoroughly. She taps it with her knuckles and is pleased that it has a slightly ringing tone. If it had an imperfection or crack, it would give off a dull flat sound. Flora and the woman bargain awhile, finally agreeing on a sum midway between the seller's first price and Flora's first offer, just as they both knew they would from the beginning.

Flora moves on to the vegetable and fruit section. This is in a large open part of the *mercado*,

Flora examines a glazed clay jug at a pottery stall.

and the sunlight falls warm and strong on the brilliant patterns of the women's clothing, and on the shining piles of fresh food. Flora passes the women selling greens—lettuce, watercress, parsley, and herbs—picked at dawn in nearby villages and still fresh and crisp. These are raised for sale to non-Indians; Indians generally don't eat salads; it is not the custom. Next to the greens are *canastas* of smooth pear-shaped *tomates*, red and soft, and next to them, heaps of fat yellow lemons, tiny green limes, knobby squashes.

Here one sees the great variety of food that can be grown in Guatemala. All kinds of produce from wheat and potatoes, which need a cool climate, to bananas and pineapples, which flourish in the heat, are raised in Guatemala. Fruits com-

mon throughout the Americas grow here, and others seldom seen in the United States—prickly pears, shaded from green to yellow to orange, and *pitahayas,* plain green outside and brilliant magenta inside, studded with tiny black seeds. Flora looks at the peaches, plums, mangoes, oranges—and stops to pick up some small sweet fruits with dusty brown skins. The bargaining is quicker here; the seller is busy with several customers and has many baskets of fruit to sell.

"*¿Cuánto cuesta?*" "How much?" asks Flora.

"*Veinte centavos la mano,*" the woman answers. "Twenty cents [for] the hand." She uses *la mano*—the hand—with its five fingers, to stand for five pieces of fruit.

"*Quinze centavos.*" "Fifteen cents," Flora offers quietly.

"*Sí,*" the woman answers and hands her the fruit.

Flora is finished with her purchases now, but before she leaves the market, she goes to the small chapel built into a corner of the walls. After the noise and hustle of the market, this place seems very dark and still. The only sound is that of a woman murmuring her prayer while she kneels in front of the brightly painted altar. Many Latin American markets have chapels, where people pray that they will sell their wares at a good price. Flora lights a candle, crosses herself, and leaves. She quickly walks the few blocks to the *parque central,* where the rest of the family have gathered.

Just as the *plazuela* is the heart of the community in San Antonio, so is the *parque central* in Antigua. The square itself is quiet and pretty.

This small chapel is right in the market.

Huge old trees shade a large fountain, flower-bordered paths, and the worn stone benches where old people doze, children play, young men watch young women, and young women watch young men.

Like others who sell regularly to tourists in the *parque*, the Hernandezes have their accustomed place. They sit on the grass and spread out the bags that Hipolitó has sewn, the shawls made in another part of the country, and the weavings Flora and Marylena and their neighbors have made. Then they watch with interest the passing parade of city happenings. The buses running between Antigua and Guatemala City load and unload on one side of the *parque central*. The *ayudantes* shout constantly to attract passengers. "*¡Guatemala! ¡Guatemala!*" they call hour after hour. Sometimes one will scramble the word for fun "*¡Malaguate! ¡Malaguate!*" On another side of the *parque* the taxi drivers are lined up, chatting to each other, polishing their cars with great

care, waiting for the tourists who travel through Antigua.

The tourists who buy from the Hernandezes come from Guatemala City, from the United States and Europe, and also from other Latin American countries. For many hours the Hernandezes may just sit without making a sale, but they see and talk with people from distant places, and this interests them.

Evelia has her own small busy world in the *parque*, which is quite different from that of her parents and Marylena. When Evelia is hungry, Flora gives her money for one of the many foods which can be bought in the *parque*. *Chuchitos* are a favorite. Evelia unwraps the husk, and bites into the warm, fragrant piece of cornmeal with its tasty tomato sauce. She also likes the fruit which is sold from a stand near the *parque*. She loves to watch the vendor take an apple or an orange, fix it between two points, and turn the small handle that spins the fruit around while a sharp blade

Top: The Hernandezes sell their cloth in Antigua.
Middle: A tasty snack—Evelia unwraps a *chuchito*.
Bottom: A vendor prepares oranges with spices.

cuts the long thin peel away. He slices the fruit in half, or in thin slices, whichever she wants, and sprinkles it with salt, cinnamon, and ground *chile*. To anyone unfamiliar with this treat, the mixture may sound startling, but the combination of the ripe juicy fruit and these spices tastes delicious to Evelia.

Much of the time Evelia and her friends pay no attention to the many activities around them. They use the *parque* as a place for their own games. They giggle at private jokes or play with Evelia's doll—feeding, dressing, putting it to bed, and then lying down beside it, just as their mothers do at home. They choose a stone bench on which to build a "fire" of discarded Popsicle sticks, with bits of grass for kindling, and cook a pretend meal there. If they feel hungry again, and if their mothers will give them the money, they run off to the boy who sells Popsicles.

"*¡Naranja, naranja, por favor!*" they say. "Orange, orange, please!" He is not much older than they are, and he has to stand up on the wheel of the cart to reach inside it, but he finds the ones they want. "*Muchas gracias*," they say, and run back to eat and play some more.

Marylena often leaves the *parque* to do errands. She goes to small workshops and stores where she can purchase things not available in the market.

The kind of pottery that the Hernandezes use is made in this workshop near the *parque central*. The building is laid out, as most city houses are, around an open courtyard where plants and flowers grow. The family who runs the business lives on one side of the courtyard, and on the others

Evelia and her friends play with their dolls, "cook" on a stone bench, and buy a Popsicle in the *parque central*.

are the pottery rooms. Here one of the workers is trimming and cleaning the pots before firing. Nearby is the kiln, a beehive-shaped structure that is fueled with wood.

A *taller*—factory or workshop—where cloth is woven is set up in much the same way, though there are more people employed here. The men work in a covered arcade that faces on the court-yard. They use a swift, much like the Hernan-dezes', and a spinning wheel to wind the hanks of thread onto bobbins for the loom. This kind of loom, like the pottery wheel, was first brought to Latin America by the Spaniards. By tradition men almost always operate these looms; they weave tablecloths and other items that are sold to wealthy Guatemalans and tourists.

This is factory work; the men are hired by the owner to work regular hours, at the same job, for a fixed amount of money. But it is a small place, and the atmosphere is relaxed. The only sounds are those of the wheels whirring softly, the regular thump of the loom, a little talk between workers, and the calls of birds flying in

and out of the flowering vines in the courtyard. These small factory shops are found throughout Latin America; they show clearly the way Latin Americans have traditionally valued a more relaxed and human work pace than is usual on assembly lines in the United States. However, in the largest Latin American cities, increasing numbers of big factories are being built, and in their emphasis on efficient mass production they are very similar to those in the United States.

Most shops in Latin American cities are also small—very different from the huge department stores in the United States. Antigua has drugstores, hardware stores, and because so many people in Antigua and the villages around it make much of their own clothing, several stores where sewing supplies are sold.

When Marylena needs some white cotton cloth for a new blouse, she goes to one of these stores near the market. The walls are piled high with bolts of cloth of many kinds. There is Dacron for lightweight men's suits, brightly colored cotton for women's dresses, toweling, sheeting, even shiny silks. Marylena looks carefully at the cotton cloth, feeling it to see that it is smooth and tightly woven. If she thinks it is too expensive, she will go to another shop, but she will not bargain with the store owner, for the prices here are fixed. When she is satisfied that she has a good piece of cloth, she pays for it and heads back to the *parque*.

By late afternoon all the Hernandezes are ready to go home. They have bought what they need, sold some of their goods, and heard much news of the world beyond San Antonio.

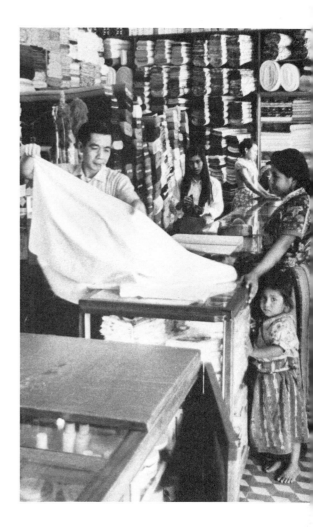

In Antigua Marylena buys cloth for a blouse.

Juegos, fiestas, y la iglesia en San Antonio— Games, Festivals, and the Church in San Antonio

Many Indians in Latin America are so poor that they must work nearly all their waking hours just to keep themselves fed, clothed, and housed. But others, like the Hernandezes and a number of their neighbors, have time, energy, and a little extra money to use for other activities. They enjoy several games and homemade amusements. And they are also able to take an active part in the rich yearly cycle of Catholic religious ceremonies and celebrations, and to care for their own village church, which is very important to them.

A favorite entertainment in San Antonio is kite flying. In November, strong winds begin to move

The family watches as Hipolitó begins to make a kite.

along the hillsides and valleys—not cold and chilling, not strong enough to harm the vegetation and thatch-roofed houses, but perfect for flying *barriletes*.

As this time approaches, most of the households with children begin to prepare for it. The small *tiendas* in San Antonio stock brightly colored tissue paper, glue, and balls of thin kite string. Those people who are expert at making *barriletes* start to buy the materials. Those who are not begin to save a little money to buy a *barrilete* from someone who makes extras to sell.

There are many traditional designs for *barriletes*, and Hipolitó knows how to make almost all of them. When he begins work, all the members of the family stop what they are doing to join in. Thin, flexible, strong sticks are gathered, and powdered glue is mixed with water into a smooth paste. Hipolitó and his young helper, Miguel, make *barriletes* with the same unhurried care and quiet attention they use when they sew. Arnoldo and Evelia, less skillful, watch very quietly, not asking questions, learning by looking, enjoying. Hipolitó and Miguel are making a kite called *mono* —monkey. First Hipolitó forms the string into a circle, holding it out with his hands and feet, and slowly inserts the four notched sticks. With great care, Miguel pastes the bright tissue paper over the frame. Then he trims the paper neatly, and attaches the streamers.

As soon as the paste is dry, he hurries into the street to try out the *barrilete*. Will it go up? It bounces about, fluttering, then clears the ground. Caught in a little breeze, it rises, just missing the

Top: Miguel pastes tissue paper over the frame.
Bottom: Success—the kite begins to fly!

stalk fences that line the lane—and then dances high up on a current. Yes, it's a fine strong *mono!*

In Latin America, religious celebrations include many entertainments, as well as the more serious church services. Indians and *ladinos* alike are nearly all Catholic, and those who are able to, celebrate the important religious days with feasts, parades, and *fiestas*. Guatemalan Indians have combined Roman Catholicism with their own ancient religions. This makes for lively ceremonies, complete with firecrackers—the grander the occasion, the more enormous the explosions—and with *marimba* music—gay rippling tunes played on the xylophonelike instrument so popular in Guatemala.

Each village in Guatemala has a patron saint and holds a yearly *fiesta* on that saint's day. This is the most important day of the year for the village. People attend the *fiesta* of their own village and also travel to those in nearby communities when they can.

The Hernandezes often go to the *fiesta* at Sumpango, a town some distance from San Antonio, for it is a very big one. They set aside their work that day, for, unlike many Indians, they can afford to lose the earnings of a day's work. With great excitement, they begin their trip, first taking a bus to Antigua, and then changing there to another bus that goes to the town where the festival is held.

When they get off the second bus, they feel taken aback for a moment. The usually quiet and orderly community is transformed, crowded with

Indians from a dozen villages and with *ladinos* from as far away as Guatemala City.

Walking toward the center of town, they begin to hear music. Evelia and Arnoldo are excited, for they already know what they will soon see. The sounds grow louder, the crowd becomes thicker—and then, high over peoples' heads, they see the *gigantes*.

These giant puppets, each carried by a man, are dancing to the music of a *marimba* band. The *marimba* players strike the wooden bars so swiftly that the mallets they hold are a blur, while the drummer and bass player keep up a steady accompaniment. The *gigantes*, as though caught up in the rhythm, bob and sway, tilt forward and back, spin suddenly, skirts belling out, long arms flying. Even Evelia knows they aren't real, but are just figures of cloth and wood—she has seen them at many *fiestas;* yet all the Hernandezes watch with fascination, enjoying the music and the dancing. Strings and strings of firecrackers explode all around them, filling the air with noise and smoke.

When the *marimba* band and the *gigante* men stop to rest, the Hernandezes move on to the fair, where two Ferris wheels have been set up for the occasion. They carry giggling groups of boys and girls high in the air, around and around. Flora and Arnoldo watch quietly, fascinated and smiling, but none of the Hernandezes choose to take the scary ride. They see the merry-go-round nearby; it is less frightening and strange, more appealing. Evelia and Arnoldo choose dappled ponies, side by side. They wait expectantly for the ride to start, then hold on tightly as the merry-go-

Top: Gigantes dance to *marimba* music at a *fiesta*.
Bottom: Flora and Arnoldo watch the Ferris wheel.

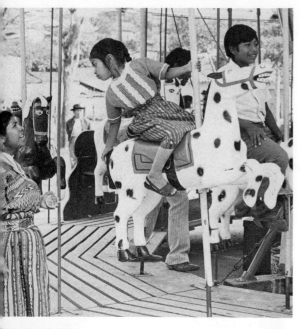

round begins to turn, slowly, then faster and faster. They laugh, calling out to Flora as they spin by, "Look, Mama, look!" The people, the *fiesta* grounds, the town, the hills around it, the blue sky, all blur in a dizzying stream of colors and patterns. Though Arnoldo is twelve, he doesn't think of the merry-go-round as something for little children—for him it is a once-a-year treat.

When the Hernandezes are hungry, they sample some of the many foods for sale. Arnoldo and Evelia particularly like chicken *tacos*. They watch with pleasure as the vendor sprinkles the crisp, chicken-stuffed *tortillas* with relish, parsley, hot sauce, and *queso*. Later they seek a woman selling soft drinks and fruit for their old favorite—sliced oranges with cinnamon, salt, and *chile* powder.

There are many games at the *fiesta*. Evelia is too shy to play them, but Arnoldo takes a try at ring-toss, and wins a prize.

Not until the sun is going down, and the Hernandezes have spent all the money they can afford, do they climb onto a bus heading for Antigua. Tired but pleased with the *fiesta* and knowing there are others to come during the year, they ride contentedly home.

The *fiesta* of San Cristobal in Antigua is another favorite of the Hernandezes. San Cristobal is the patron saint of travelers, and Antigua, as a popular tourist center, has a large number of taxis and buses, conveyances for travelers. On this day they are all decorated with signs, religious figures, masses of flowers, and fluttering paper streamers. A contest

Arnoldo and Evelia enjoy the *fiesta*.

is held in the *parque central* to judge the most beautiful one, and afterward, their hoods are opened and their engines carefully blessed by a priest. Here a young man has joined the parade of vehicles with a homemade airplane loaded with passengers and under full bicycle power!

In San Antonio and many other Indian villages, church activities are the main way in which large numbers of people come together; they feel that the church belongs to them, and they work hard to take care of it. All contributions to the church from the people of San Antonio are handled by a committee, which pays Padre Frank small sums of money for special services and decides how best to use the rest. The village does not pay Padre Frank's salary, but it does pay for the maintenance of the church building. Members of the church take turns looking after it, keeping fresh flowers on the altar, cleaning and dressing the statues of the saints. They even follow the traditional custom of appointing someone to guard the church by sleeping in it every night.

In addition, for each of the important Catholic holidays observed in San Antonio, there is a group that makes all the arrangements for the celebration. On these days large powerful firecrackers are set off in the *plazuela* early in the morning. As the smoke rises, the sound echoes back and forth between the hills. Two men and a boy play traditional Indian music on drums and a clay flute. These old Mayan tunes, so different from Spanish music, are another example of the way the Indians have remembered their own customs and blended them with those of the Spaniards.

Top: A bicycle-powered plane at a *fiesta* parade.
Bottom: Music and firecrackers mark a celebration.

The villagers also hold a religious ceremony whenever a new building is completed. Here a family has decorated an addition to their house with tissue-paper streamers and sprinkled fresh pine needles on the floor. They have set up a small altar, with candles, flowers, and incense—the same kind of incense, *copal*, that their Mayan ancestors used in religious ceremonies. When Padre Frank arrives to bless the structure, as many strings of firecrackers as the family can afford are set off. The family kneels while the padre says prayers, asks for God's blessing on the new building, and sprinkles it with holy water.

Every Sunday morning Padre Frank comes to say Mass in San Antonio. As a man rings the church bells, people begin to leave their homes and head for the *plazuela*. The Hernandezes and their neighbors hurry, for though the church is the largest building in San Antonio, it is not nearly big enough to hold everyone who attends Mass. Those who cannot get in stand outdoors,

Top: Padre Frank blesses a new building in San Antonio.
Bottom: A woman covers her head as she enters church.

the men on one side and the women on the other, and listen to Padre Frank's voice over the loudspeaker. From time to time his sentences are interrupted by the noise of firecrackers in the *plazuela.*

Inside, the church is crowded but quiet. Babies sleep, tied snugly to their mothers' backs, or nurse if they are hungry. Little children kneel solemnly beside their parents and join in whatever responses they know. The murmuring voices echo in the tall old building, just as they have nearly every Sunday for more than four hundred years.

The last church ceremony for every San Antonio person is the funeral Mass. Most of the people who are born in San Antonio live out their lives here and die here. For some, life is short—many babies die, many children, many young adults.

Lacking adequate medical care, lacking enough nourishing food, they die from infectious diseases that are only minor illnesses in a richer society. Others, like Emilio Santos, though worn by long years of hard work, live to be very old.

All are buried in the San Antonio cemetery, just a short walk from the *plazuela*, down narrow lanes fenced with cornstalks, past *café* bushes growing in the soft light of tall shade trees. The *cementerio* is a quiet, peaceful place, surrounded by fields of corn and beans, vegetables, fruits and flowers, and ringed by the hills. The only sounds here are bird calls and the wind moving through the trees and grass.

The graves of the poorer people are marked by small weather-beaten wooden crosses, and those of the wealthier, by brightly painted tombs. Old family names appear over and over—Lopez, Hernandez, Martinez, Santos. The markers are dated

yesterday, fifty years ago, one hundred years ago; the oldest are too worn to read.

Many generations of San Antonio people are buried here; generations of farmers and weavers, people who worked and lived long ago in ways similar to those of Hipolitó and Flora, Marylena, Arnoldo, and Evelia today. Change has been slow; life under the Spanish has been hard; but the people of San Antonio endure.

When Marylena, Arnoldo, and Evelia's grandparents were children, their world was small. They never traveled more than fifty miles from home. Their Spanish was very limited, so they talked mainly with others who spoke Cakchiquel like themselves.

Marylena, Arnoldo, Evelia, and the generation to which they belong are learning the skills and beliefs of their grandparents, for their Indian heritage is important and valuable to them. They are also learning about the world beyond San Antonio. They can read and write Spanish, the official language of their country. They have traveled to many parts of Guatemala. They listen to news of the whole world on the radio. They exchange letters with foreigners they have met in Antigua.

Their world is expanding: there will be new problems, and there will be new opportunities. And there will be a chance for them to maintain a life of their own—their own traditions and their pride in being Indian.

Taller—

Workshop

Welcome to the workshop. As we told you in the beginning, this book is something you can use to understand and to start to feel a little of what it's like to be an Indian in Latin America. You could think of these last pages as a shop full of hammers, nails, saws, wire, and glue from which you can construct your own understandings. These tools, together with the ones you already have—your mind and your body—can be used anywhere—at home, at school, or in a playground with your friends.

As you carry out some of these projects and experiments, give your attention to what you are experiencing in your body. Are your muscles working harder than they need to? Are some muscles not working at all? Are some quick to get tired or tense? Do you frown, smile, whistle, sigh, feel alive or sluggish? Do you sometimes hold your breath? How do you feel when you concentrate, or when you try something you've never tried before, or when you become bored?

Perhaps you would like to keep a journal of the feelings, experiences, and thoughts that you have while doing these experiments.

The Hernandezes' Compound

You can get a feeling of what the Hernandez home is like by laying out the shape of their compound on a vacant lot or on a paved part of your schoolyard or playground. On the vacant lot you can put sticks in the ground and tie strings around them to represent the shapes of the compound and rooms, and on pavement you can draw the shapes with chalk. Make the layout life-size, so you can walk around in it. The dimensions are marked on the drawing by Arnoldo. If you are using chalk on asphalt, you can crosshatch the areas that are roofed to get an idea of how much of the compound is open and how much is closed. When you stand in the *cocina*, think about what it would be like for six or seven people to eat breakfast

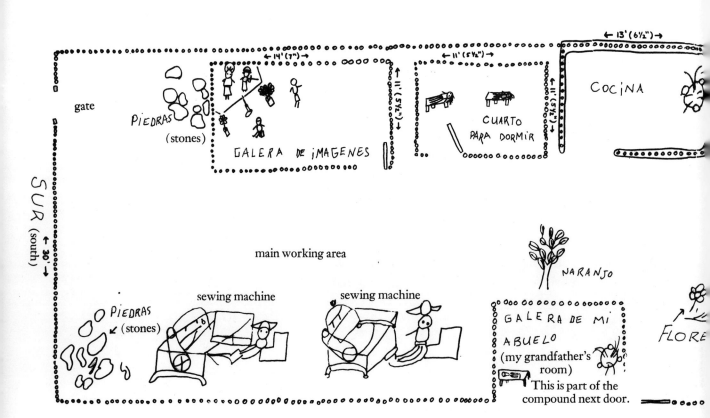

there. You might try sitting down in it with a small group, but be careful not to burn yourselves in the fire!

If you like, you can make a scale model of the Hernandezes' compound. Before you begin, look through the book and study carefully all the photographs of the compound, as well as the drawing below made by Arnoldo.

You will need to make a box 15 inches wide and 60 inches long, with sides about 4 inches high. This box represents the compound. In a model of this size, 1 inch of the box stands for 2 feet of the compound. You can make your container by cutting and putting together discarded cardboard cartons of the sort you get from a supermarket. The amount of cutting and taping or gluing you have to do will depend on the size of the cartons

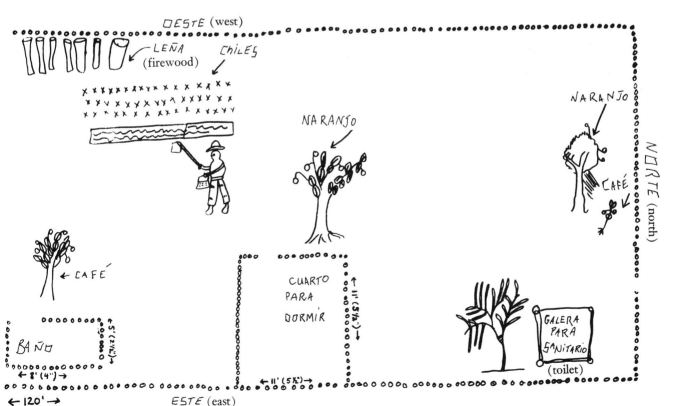

you use. Put a layer of earth about 1½ inches deep in the bottom of the box and press it down firmly and evenly. Make the dirt higher at the end farthest from the gate, so that the ground slopes, as it does in the actual compound. You may want to line the box with plastic or newspaper so that the dirt doesn't leak out.

For the walls of the rooms you can use pieces of cardboard or, even better, wooden matchsticks or twigs stuck into the earthen floor. You will find the dimensions of the rooms for this scale model in parentheses on the drawing. Pieces of cardboard with grass pasted on them can be roofs, or you could use aluminum foil shaped to look like the corrugated aluminum that is used for roofs in Guatemala. You can even put in small plants, to represent those that are shown in the drawing. Be sure to include the three-rock cooking area in the *cocina*.

Sweeping

Probably you've begun to realize that the Indians of Guatemala have few of the labor-saving appliances you and your family may own or use. Daily chores take longer and require more effort for people like the Hernandezes than for you. You can learn something about these differences by acting out a few of their daily chores. You might begin with sweeping.

There are two types of Guatemalan brooms you can make. For the one the man is using, gather some 2-foot-long flexible branches from a tree or bush. The branches from palms are best, and are

most like the ones the Hernandezes would use, but branches from other trees or bushes or long grasses will do. Attach them with twine to the end of a 4-foot pole. In Guatemala they use cane stalks for handles, but you can use an old broom or mop handle. To make a broom like the one the woman is holding, cut the branches longer to begin with. Arrange them so that the heavy parts of the branches are at one end, where you can tie them together to form a handle.

Now try sweeping various surfaces, such as your porch, driveway, or the sidewalk in front of your home. Sweep one half of your driveway or sidewalk with your handmade broom. Time yourself to see how long it takes. Remember how it feels—how your hands feel holding the handle, how hard or easy it is to brush the bristles over the ground, which muscles work. Then sweep the other half with a store-bought broom, again timing yourself. Think about how that feels—and about how much faster a vacuum cleaner does this kind of work.

Carrying with a Head Pad

As you saw earlier in the book, women are able to carry great loads balanced on the tops of their heads using a head pad. If you would like to experience what Flora and Marylena feel like when they go to the *pila* for water or to the *molino* to have the day's corn ground, begin by making a head pad.

The head pad is made by folding a *tsute* into a loose ropelike shape. For a *tsute*, you will need a piece of cotton cloth measuring about 34 inches

by 45 inches. An old sheet cut to that size will work fine. Look at the photographs and copy the folds shown. You should end up with a long narrow cloth. Holding the narrower tip between your thumb and palm, wrap the *tsute* around your hand until you have a firm coil. Stick the tag end in between the last two layers.

Spend some time finding the place where the pad sits best on your head. Practice walking around with just the pad on your head until you get used to having it there. When you feel comfortable with it, and fairly sure it won't slide off, try carrying various nonbreakable containers—a plastic or aluminum mixing bowl would be excellent. The container should have something in it, to give it enough weight to sit firmly on the pad. Maybe you have some clay or a package of dried beans

you can use. You might want to weigh your container with its load, and while you're walking around with it on your head, remember that Marylena often carries loads of over a hundred pounds. Also remember that she's been doing this kind of carrying for a long time, and when she was learning, she started with very small loads.

Carrying Babies

Indian babies are carried everywhere by their mothers, sometimes until they are several years old. When Evelia was a baby, she was carried in a *tsute* on Flora's back.

The photograph of Estrella on the next page shows how the *tsute* is arranged. You can try carrying a doll or a stuffed animal this way. Or, with

your mother's permission and help, you might want to try carrying a younger brother or sister.

To load the baby, keep your back straight and bend over from the hips. Place the child on your back with its head facing up and its tummy against your body. Place the *tsute* over the child, bringing one corner over your right shoulder and one corner under your left arm. Pull the cloth tightly and tie it over your chest. Stand up slowly, tucking in and adjusting the cloth to support and balance the child. If you are carrying a real baby, give your attention to how you breathe while you load and carry and how your back and legs and neck feel.

Washing Clothes

How much time do most people in the United States spend washing a load of dirty clothes? Perhaps it takes two minutes to put the clothes in the washer, two minutes to move them into the dryer when they are clean, and ten minutes to fold and put them away. The rest of the time is spent waiting, at home or in a laundromat. You can watch and time someone, or ask how long it takes.

Flora works steadily for about an hour at her washing. You can read the description of how she does her laundry on page 9. If you want to learn something of what it's like to wash clothes the way Flora does, try the following experiment.

You will need an old-fashioned washboard, or a piece of finished wood, a big bucket of water, and a bar of soap. You will also need a small mixing bowl to scoop water out of the bucket. In

Estrella uses one *tsute* for a head pad, and another to hold her child.

this experiment, the bucket takes the place of the public water supply, the *pila*. The small bowl is like the one Flora uses, and the washboard is a substitute for the slanted slab at the *pila*.

It might be best to try Flora's washing method outside, but you can also try it inside in your bathtub or laundry tub. Arrange the washboard so that it is at a slight angle. If you are outside, you can prop up one end with some good-sized stones. Kneel behind the higher end of the board and place one piece of clothing on the washboard. Inspect the cloth you are about to wash and remember where the dirty spots are. Later you must check again to see if you have scrubbed it clean.

Using the small bowl, scoop some clear water out of your bucket and pour it over the clothing on the board until it is thoroughly wet. Next take a bar of soap and rub it vigorously all over the wet clothing. Now rub the piece you are washing up and down across the ridges of the washboard. Keep doing this, turning the clothing over frequently, until it is clean and you are ready to rinse out the soap.

Since your bucket is really the *pila*, when you are rinsing you must be very careful to prevent any soap from getting into the bucket. Remember that the *pila* supplies water for all village activities, and that if you spill soap into it, your noonday meal may taste a bit sudsy. With the small bowl, scoop the water from the bucket in such a way that your soapy hand does not touch the water in the bucket. When you pour the fresh water from the small bowl over the soapy clothing, do it so that the water first drains over your hands, rinsing them, then falls on the clothing. Continue to scoop and rinse until the clothing is free of soap, adding fresh water to the bucket as you need it. Squeeze the cloth and spread it out on the grass, on a bush, or over a line to dry.

If you have several washboards, set them up in a row so that three or four friends can wash at the same time. If you laugh and talk a lot, you will be even more like Flora washing.

A Dishcloth

Washing dishes probably takes Marylena and Flora longer than it takes you. They must go to the *pila* and carry back water, and now and then they have to make their own dishcloths. Their method, however, does little harm to the environment. No fuel is used—they wash with cold water. No electricity is used—they don't have a dishwasher or garbage disposal as do many families in the United States. There is nothing harmful to the soil in the leftover water—they use organic, biodegradable bar soap instead of detergent, and their dishcloth is a dried cornhusk, which when thrown away, becomes part of the soil.

A Guatemalan dishcloth is simple to make. All you need is an ear of corn and some time. Choose a piece of corn with a complete husk, including a short piece of stem. Carefully pull back the sections of the husk, one at a time, so that it remains in one piece. Remove the ear of corn and the silk.

Hang the husk up to dry in a sunny window or over a heater in your house. About a week in

The dishwashing area in the Hernandezes' compound.

the sun is enough. When it is thoroughly dried—it will turn yellow-tan—slit each piece of the husk along its length into very thin strips or strings. You can do this either with your fingernail, as Marylena would do it, or with a small knife. As you slit the husk, be careful not to tear it off the stem, so that your dishcloth will be in one piece. If you use your fingernail, pay attention to how your fingers feel as the husk slides through them. How do they feel after you have finished making the dishcloth?

You are now ready to wash dishes. Wet the cornhusk and rub it with soap, as you would any other dishcloth. If you are pleased with the way this one works, you may want to convert your family to using cornhusk cloths. Once cornhusks are dry, they can easily be stored, so all you have to do is save up a supply when fresh corn is in season.

Bathing

The Hernandezes use water carefully, so as to make as few trips to the *pila* as possible. One of the ways they conserve water is to use only a little when they take a bath, and you can find out what one of their baths is like very easily. Take two unbreakable bowls to your bathtub or shower. Each bowl should hold about two quarts. Fill both with cold water and set them on the floor of the tub or shower. Stand in the tub and wash yourself all over with soap and the water from one bowl. The Hernandezes use a cornhusk washcloth—the same kind they use for dishwashing. After you have

lathered and scrubbed yourself, rinse yourself off with the water that is left in the first bowl, then rinse again very carefully with the clear water in the second bowl. No fair adding water to either bowl.

Weaving

The looms used by the women of San Antonio are very complicated, but you can make a simple loom that will give you an idea of what it's like to do backstrap loom weaving. You can even make a belt or a headband on it.

You will need seven Popsicle sticks or tongue depressors, though pieces of strong cardboard will work if cut about the same size. You will also need white glue and yarn or string. Drill holes in the centers of five of the sticks and glue the sticks together, so they look like the heddle in the photograph.

Cut nine pieces of string or yarn about 12 inches longer than the length of whatever you want to make. Tie all the strings together by knotting them at one end, and attach the knot to a nail or hook or to a doorknob about 4 feet from the floor. Pull the strings through the heddle—one through each hole and one through each slot. Once the strings are in place, bunch them together, make another knot, and tie them somehow to yourself. You can tie them to another piece of string which then ties around your waist, or invent your own method.

Kneel on the floor. Weave by lifting the heddle and sliding a piece of yarn across between

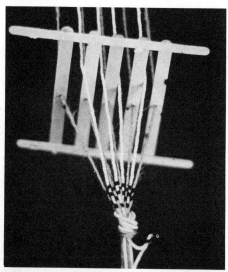

Top: Maximina weaves near a stack of drying firewood.
Middle: A Popsicle loom.
Bottom: Separate the warp by raising the heddle.

the two sets of strings, which are the warp threads. Then lower the heddle and send the yarn back through the two sets of warp threads in the opposite direction. Continue until the weaving is as long as you want it.

If you want to change colors, just tie the new colored string to the old one and keep on going.

Pay particular attention to your knees, back, and shoulders. As you work, remember that Marylena and Flora are able to do this kind of weaving for hours. In fact, the cash supply of many families depends on a woman working at a loom for many hours, almost every day.

WAIST STRING

Preparing and Planting Chile Seeds

You might gain a clearer understanding of the farming conditions for Indians in Guatemala by working on this project and the three following ones.

To prepare your own *chile* seeds, buy a few *chiles*, either red or green, from your grocer. Tie one end of a long string around the stem of a pepper. Leave a little space on the string, and tie it around the next pepper. When all the peppers are tied, hang the string in a sunny window or over a stove. If it is very damp where you live, cut the *chiles* into quarters before stringing them. This will help prevent them from mildewing. When the *chiles* are quite dry and the flesh is hard and brittle, slit each one open and remove the seeds. Save the skins—they can be ground into a very fine *chile* powder and used for seasoning.

You can raise peppers from seeds you prepare

Top: Tie the strings from the loom to another piece of string.
Bottom: David Lopez removes seeds from dried *chiles*.

yourself, or from those bought from a store, if you have a sunny window or yard. Prepare a small plot of ground, or fill a flower pot or wooden box with earth. Scatter the seeds on the surface and cover them with a thin layer of earth. Be sure to keep the soil moist until the seeds sprout. When they are about 2 inches high, thin the seedlings, so that they are at least 6 inches apart, and water them whenever the earth is dry. When the peppers are full grown, you can harvest and dry them. You can use them, fresh or dry, to make the hot sauce on page 108. Be sure to save some seeds, as Hipolitó does, to plant next year's crop!

Planting Maíz

There probably isn't a market near your home where you can buy a *quintal* of *maíz* and carry it home with a tumpline. However, you can go to a store and buy a package of corn seed. Follow the directions on the package for planting corn in your area. If you would like to compare some different methods of growing *maíz*, you will need to prepare three different patches of ground.

If you want to plant corn the way Hipolitó does, and have a yard or other outdoor place in which to work, find the steepest slope you can. Turn over the soil on one half of your intended patch, and plant the *maíz* in rows that go across the slope.

The government in Guatemala is trying to teach the farmers to make terraces on which to grow their *maíz*. If you would like to try this method, prepare the other half of your patch dif-

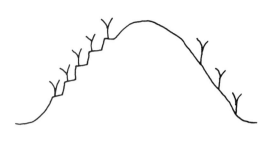

ferently. Make a series of steps as shown in the drawing, and plant your seeds on the top of each step.

Prepare and plant a third patch on level ground. If you plant the seeds on the three patches at the same time, you can compare them at all stages of growth. Notice how much water is absorbed and how much runs off. Note the amount of topsoil that washes away. Does the corn on all three patches sprout at the same time? Do the plants on each patch grow at about the same rate? If any of your plants die, which patch or patches are they on? Notice the differences in how your body feels working on the slope and on level ground.

Experimenting with Erosion

Soil depletion and erosion are very serious problems for farmers everywhere. There are many experiments you can perform on the causes, speed, and effects of erosion. A few are listed here.

Before you begin your experiments, gather the following materials: soil, three shoe boxes, one roll of aluminum foil, a knife, a watering can with a sprinkler head, a measuring cup, and three 8- or 10-ounce drinking glasses.

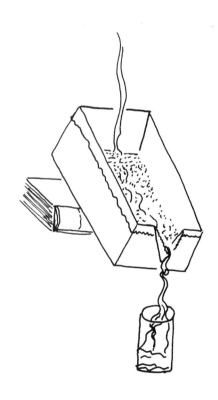

Cut a large V in one end of each of the shoe boxes. Line each box with aluminum foil, forming a spout with the foil in the V-end of the box. Fill the three boxes with soil. Using books or stones, raise the closed end of one box about 1 inch, the next box about 3½ inches, and the last box about 6 inches. Place a drinking glass under each spout. Water the soil of each box hard. What

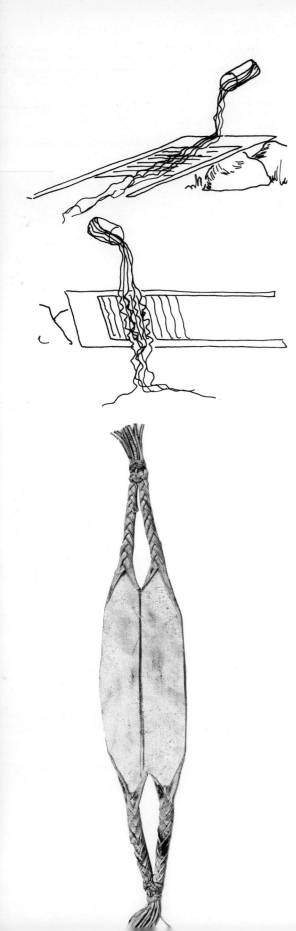

happens? When you compare your results you will have an idea about how the steepness of a slope effects the loss of soil.

Terracing

The faster water goes down a slope, the more topsoil it carries along. Terracing helps to slow down the water by making it go over small step-like plots down a steep hillside. You can test the speed of water running down a slope by using a washboard and a watch with a second hand. Prop up the washboard so that one end is about a foot off the ground and the ridges in the board are parallel with the ground. Now the washboard is like a terraced hillside. Pour a certain amount of water on the high end of the board and record the time it takes for the water to reach the ground. Then turn the washboard on its side so that the ridges are perpendicular to the ground. Prop up one side a foot and pour the same amount of water on the high end. Again measure the time it takes for the water to reach the ground. This may give you an idea of how planting on terraces allows the soil to hold water and slows down erosion.

A Tumpline

When Hipolitó brings home a *quintal* of *maíz* from Antigua, he uses a tumpline that crosses his forehead to carry much of the weight of the load while the sack itself rests on his back. If you think you'd like to try this kind of carrying, look carefully at this picture of the headband of the tumpline.

To make the headband, begin with a piece of heavy leather 24 inches long and 4 inches wide. If you don't have any heavy leather, you can cut your headband out of canvas or any strong cloth.

Cut two 8-inch-long slits in the leather or cloth as shown in the drawing and separate the "legs" at both ends. Cut two 7-inch-long slits in each of the four legs, so that each leg is made up of three strands.

Braid each leg to within 3 inches of the end. Then braid two legs together, pairing the strands as shown so that you are making a braid with six strands. Wrap tightly with heavy twine about 1 inch from the end of the cloth. Do the same with the other two legs.

Insert a 10- to 12-foot-long rope between the legs as shown in the drawing. When you carry a load, the headband should lie across your hairline with the braided legs either behind, over, or in front of your ears. Hold the loose ends of the rope in your hands and have a friend adjust the loop around your load. When the load is in place, you can either tie the rope ends to the tumpline legs or hold them with your hands.

When you first begin to carry a load with a tumpline, do not transport anything that is too heavy or that is breakable. Twenty to thirty pounds would be a good weight to begin with. You may want to pack your load into a cardboard box or a large laundry bag. Try to imagine what it would be like to carry a typical Indian's load—a hundred pounds—for several miles.

A tumpline can be strung on a back-pack and used along with the pack's regular straps. The

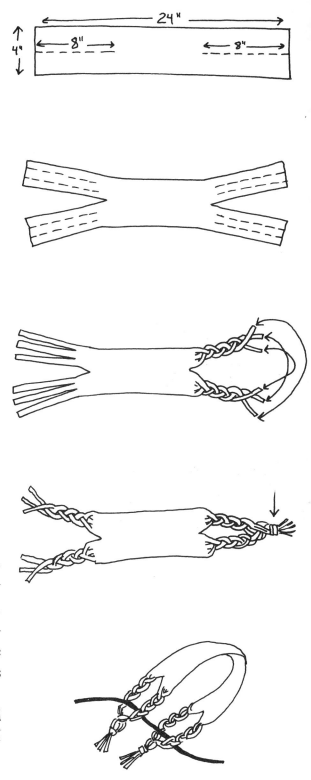

tumpline helps to distribute the weight of the pack more evenly and is especially useful when you go on a long hike.

Cooking

One of the most unchanging aspects of life in Indian Guatemala is the menu for the main meal. Except on special occasions, this meal consists of *frijoles negros* and *tortillas*. If a family can afford it, they buy a small portion of a locally made cheese, which is somewhat like cream cheese. When you think about eating this meal for dinner every day of the year, you might imagine you'd be bored with it. You're probably right. In the United States, people are accustomed to having a great variety of foods. They may eat much the same breakfast every day, but don't want their dinner to be repetitious. People in the United States have been brought up to value things that are new and different, while the Hernandezes and their neighbors have been raised in another tradition. It does not occur to the Hernandez family to be bored with their unchanging main meal. They expect to have *frijoles* and *tortillas* every day, because that is what they've always had.

If you would like to try eating a typical Hernandez meal, you can easily prepare it at home or at school.

FRIJOLES

The *frijoles* used in Guatemala are small and black. In the United States you can probably buy them at health food stores, or at markets in Spanish-American neighborhoods. If you can't buy *frijoles negros*, use dried pinto or kidney beans.

1. Cover 1 cup dried *frijoles* with cold water and soak for several hours or overnight.

2. Add a few green onions or half a yellow onion cut fine, a teaspoon of salt, and more water to cover the beans again, and simmer covered over a low heat for three hours or till the *frijoles* are very tender. Be sure to check every twenty minutes to see if you need to add more water. As they cook, the *frijoles* soak up the water in the pot.

3. Make the *frijoles* into a paste by grinding them through a food mill or ricer, or by mashing them with a potato masher.

4. Put the mashed *frijoles* in a serving bowl and serve hot.

With this amount of *frijoles* you can thinly cover 14 *tortillas*. Two cups of dried *frijoles* when cooked should thinly cover 28 *tortillas*. You can also eat and enjoy these *frijoles* without *tortillas*.

TORTILLAS

You can buy these frozen, canned, and sometimes fresh. Whatever kind you buy, wrap them in aluminum foil and heat them in the oven until they are hot and steamy. Serve them in a basket or dish lined and covered with a cloth to keep them warm.

If you wish to make your own fresh *tortillas*, you may be able to buy the special corn flour you need in a supermarket. (Regular cornmeal will not work.) One brand you can use, put out

by the Quaker Oats Company, is called Masa Harina. Follow the directions on the package.

After you have patted your *tortillas* you may want to make their thicknesses a little more even. Put them between two pieces of waxed paper and press down gently with a piece of cardboard.

HOT SAUCE

You can make a chili sauce by cooking together until soft, chopped onions, chopped fresh or canned tomatoes, and chopped fresh hot peppers (or a little chili powder). If you have grown your own *chiles*, according to the suggestions on pages 101–102, use them fresh or dried for this sauce. Make chili powder from the dried *chiles* by crushing them with a rolling pin.

QUESO

Put a square of cream cheese on a plate and bring it to the table.

Eating this meal is very simple. Put about one or two tablespoons of *frijoles* in the middle of the *tortilla*. Add several small lumps of *queso*, and roll up the *tortilla*. Add a little hot sauce if you like.

A Market

The largest number of people you can find is the right amount for a Guatemalan market. A school class or two would be perfect. Sit down together and read the chapter on the market. Talk about the kinds of things you will sell at your market, and be sure to have a big variety. Remember that almost everything, from hair ribbons to medicine for

Produce is weighed in a balance scale.

chickens, can be found at a Guatemalan market. You and your classmates need to think about who you are, what you raise or make for sale, and what you need to buy from each other. You might even set yourselves specific goals—like pretending you must sell four eggs and three bunches of onions for enough money to buy some rice and a few *tomates*.

You also need to plan when people will be buyers and when they will be sellers. Most sellers will need a small rug or mat, or maybe a table. Some sellers can walk around among the stalls, calling out what wares they have for sale. Each seller will have to decide the asking price and the lowest selling price that is acceptable for the goods he or she sells. Furthermore, the seller must decide how to sell the goods, whether by the pound with a balance scale, by the *mano* (see page 70), or so many for a certain amount—*seis por cinco centavos*, six for five cents. The seller will need coins to make change, and the buyer, of course, will need them to buy. The Guatemalan money system includes the following:

One quetzal (paper bill) = $1.00
½ quetzal (paper bill) = $ .50
20 centavos (coin) = $ .20
10 centavos (coin) = $ .10
5 centavos (coin) = $ .05
1 centavo (coin) = $ .01

Because prices are very low in Guatemala, and most people have little money, paper bills are seldom used in a market. If you like, you can do some research and draw copies of the actual Guate-

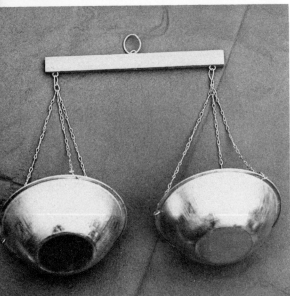

malan bills. Tokens or cardboard disks make fine coins.

If you have a long time to prepare for your market, you may want to make some clay pots —pinch or coil pots are easiest—tumplines, woven belts, stick or grass brooms, and some *petate* mats. Look back through the book and see how many things you can find that you can sell in your market.

In case you are going to sell your goods by weight, here are directions for constructing a balance scale. Before you begin, take a careful look at the scales the woman is holding. You will need:

One piece of 1- × 1-inch wood about 10 inches long
Three small screw eyes
One metal ring
Two round aluminum-foil pans (like the ones small frozen chicken pies come in) or round plastic margarine containers
Sturdy twine

1. Measure carefully to find the center of your piece of wood and screw a screw eye into it at this point. Insert the ring in the screw eye and squeeze it closed.
2. Working on the *other* side of the wood—opposite the side the ring is on—measure in and make a mark ¾ inch from each end. Carefully screw in one screw eye at each mark.
3. Make three holes near the rim of each pie tin. The holes should be approximately the same distance apart. Thread a piece of twine about 10 inches long through each hole and tie it in place.

Then tie the three pieces of twine to one of the screw eyes at the end of the piece of wood. Tie the other pie tin in the same way, making sure that the two pie tins hang the same distance below the wood so that you can easily tell when your scale is in balance.

4. Find an object or several objects that make one pound. You can measure your pound on a postage scale or on a vegetable scale in a supermarket or grocery store. This will be your standard: put it in one pan. Slowly fill the other pan with whatever you want to weigh, until both pans balance. Be sure you are holding the scale by the ring and not by the wood. When the pans balance, you know the object or objects in the second pan weigh one pound.

There are several possible places to hold your market. Indoors, a basement or a classroom with the desks pushed aside is fine. Outdoors, you can use a vacant lot, backyard, or playground. Indian markets are very crowded, so try to pick a space that is not too large for the number of participants.

As you know, bargaining is the method of establishing a price. Indian bargaining is very polite and quiet, and there is no arguing. Before your market you might practice some of these phrases, so that you can carry out your bargaining in Spanish.

Good morning. *Buenos días.*
How are you? *¿Cómo está usted?*
Fine, thank you. *Bien, gracias.*

And you? *¿Y usted?*

I want. *Yo quiero.*

Do you have? *¿Tiene usted?*

How much? *¿Cuántos?*

How much does it cost? *¿Cuánto questa?*

How much are they? *¿Cuántos son?*

It is too expensive. *Eso es demasiado.*

They are very cheap. *Son muy baratos.*

Do you have change? *¿Tiene usted cambio?*

I don't have change. *No tengo cambio.*

OK, indicating a sale is agreed upon. *Bueno,* or *Vaya.*

pound *libra*

hand *mano*

each one *cada un*

NUMEROS

1	*uno*	18	*dieciocho*
2	*dos*	19	*diecinueve*
3	*tres*	20	*veinte*
4	*cuatro*	21	*veintiuno*
5	*cinco*	22	*veintidós*
6	*seis*	23	*veintitrés*
7	*siete*	30	*treinta*
8	*ocho*	31	*treinta y uno*
9	*nueve*	32	*treinta y dos*
10	*diez*	40	*cuarenta*
11	*once*	41	*cuarenta y uno*
12	*doce*	42	*cuarenta y dos*
13	*trece*	50	*cincuenta*
14	*catorce*	51	*cincuenta y uno*
15	*quince*	52	*cincuenta y dos*
16	*dieciséis*	60	*sesenta*
17	*diecisiete*	61	*sesenta y uno*

62	*sesenta y dos*	81	*ochenta y uno*
70	*setenta*	90	*noventa*
71	*setenta y uno*	91	*noventa y uno*
72	*setenta y dos*	92	*noventa y dos*
80	*ochenta*	100	*ciento (cien* before a noun)

If you have made food to sell, you will have a lot on hand after your market is over. Perhaps you will want to prepare a feast. While you are sharing your meal, you might talk about the market —what it was like, how it was the same as or different from the way you and your family earn a living and buy the things you need.

Barriletes

In October and November, *cuando mucho aire*, boys and men of all ages make *barriletes*. They work slowly, delicately, and it takes them several hours to make one kite. The drawings show the most common styles of *barriletes* in San Antonio.

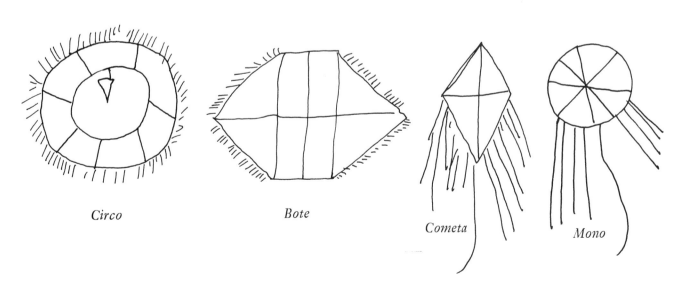

Circo   Bote   Cometa   Mono

If you look on page 77, you will find Hipolitó and Miguel constructing a *mono*. The directions here are for the same *mono*. If you want to make one larger or smaller, change the length of the sticks. After you have constructed the *mono*, you can try making the other kites shown in the drawings. Simply vary the lengths and positions of the sticks that form the frames.

For this *mono* you will need four sticks 12 inches long, kite string, four sheets of tissue paper in different colors, and glue. You will have to look around your home or neighborhood for the sticks. They must be lightweight, straight, fairly thin, and sturdy. Very thin dowels, balsa wood, bamboo sticks of the sort used for gardening, old kite parts, or fairly straight tree branches are all possible frame materials.

Make a small slit in both ends of each stick. Tie two of the sticks together in the center and open them to make a cross. With a piece of string about 4 feet long, make a slipknot, and then open the loop and stretch it around your feet. Insert the cross into the loop by letting the string wedge down into the slits. Pull the end of the string so that there is only a little slack in the loop. Miguel holds this end in his teeth. Next, add the remaining two sticks, spacing them evenly; remove your feet, and tighten the string to hold the sticks in

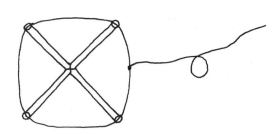

place. Tie the string tightly so it will not come loose. With another piece of string, wrap the center joint so that all four sticks are held together firmly.

Miguel measures each pie-shaped piece of tissue paper by laying the kite frame over a corner of the tissue. Then he cuts the curved, outside edge of the pie shape about ¾ inch beyond the string. Cut three more pie-shaped pieces in the same way, each from different color paper. Use a little glue to join them together along their straight edges so that they form a circle. When the glue is dry, lay the kite frame on top of the circle of tissue paper. Carefully fold the curved edges of the paper over the string and glue the flap down to the paper and sticks.

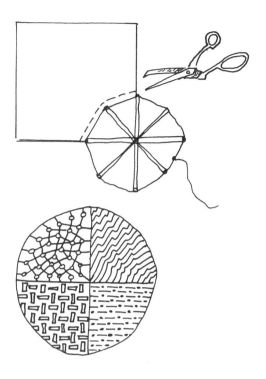

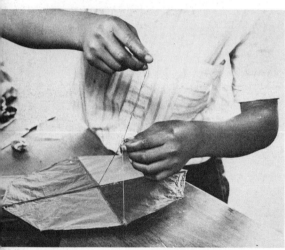

Now you are ready to make the two *flacos*, the *cola*, and the bridle. To make the first *flaco*, cut four pieces of different colored tissue paper, each about 6 × 5 inches. Lay the pieces out and glue them together along their 6-inch sides, so that they look like step 1 in the photograph. Repeat this procedure to make the second *flaco*. When the glue has dried, carefully fold over the papers four or five times and cut them into narrow strips, leaving about one third of the top piece of paper uncut, as shown in step 2 in the photograph. When you unfold the *flacos*, they should look like the one in step 3. Glue them to the *barrilete*.

For the *cola*, use a piece of crepe paper about 1½ inches wide and 36 inches long. Attach it between the two *flacos* as shown.

The bridle, the triangle of string that controls the kite in flight, is attached on the side where the sticks don't show, and is opposite the *cola*. Each of three strings is drawn through the tissue paper with a needle and then tied to the sticks, as shown in the drawing. Hold the three strings up to form a pyramid, and tie them together. Attach as much string to the bridle as you want to fly your *barrilete*.

Take it out *cuando mucho aire*, for then *es el tiempo para barriletes!*

A Fiesta

Every *fiesta* is a grand display of sounds—the *marimba*, firecrackers, flute and drum music, and hand noisemakers. *Fiestas* have special tastes—

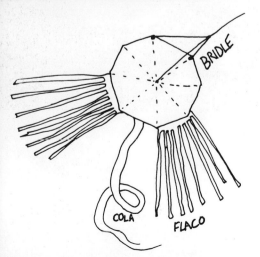

tacos, roast corn, orange slices, and candy; and they have unusual sights—floats, *gigantes*, dances, and *piñatas*.

If you would like to have a *fiesta*, you can choose to make all or some of the projects we suggest. The more people that take part in it, the more like a real *fiesta* it will be.

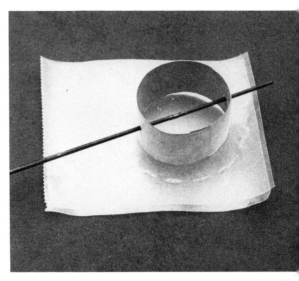

A HAND NOISEMAKER

This is a small, drumlike toy. To make it, you will need cardboard, masking tape, white glue, a stapler, a thin wooden stick or dowel about 12 inches long, waxed paper, an art gum or pink eraser, a needle, some heavy thread, and tissue paper.

Cut a piece of cardboard 1½ inches wide and 9½ inches long. Bend it into a ring, overlap the ends, and tape and staple them together. Make two holes opposite each other in the sides of the ring and glue in the stick or dowel. It should extend about 1½ inches beyond the top of the card-board.

Cut out four waxed-paper circles that are about ½ inch larger all around than the ring. Lay two of the circles on top of one open side of the ring, fold the edges down, and tape them to the card-board. Do the same on the other side. Make the waxed paper as smooth and tight as you can.

Next carve out two pea-sized hunks of eraser, and using a needle, run a thread through one. Make a knot so that the thread won't pull all the way through, and cut off the thread about 3 inches beyond the eraser. Do the same with the other hunk of eraser. Tape the threads to each

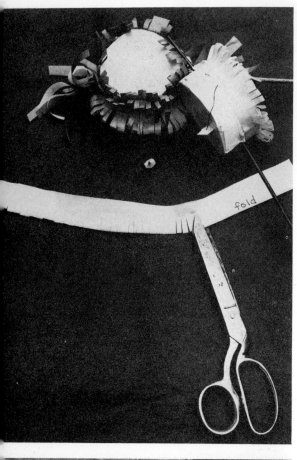

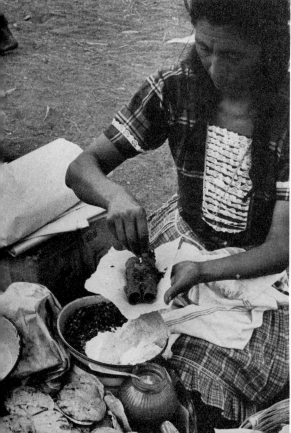

side of the ring so that the eraser can just reach the center of the waxed-paper drum head.

Decorate your hand drum with tissue paper. You can invent your own design. If you want to make decorations like those in the photograph, cut a strip of tissue paper 2 inches wide and 12 inches long. Fold it in half lengthwise, so it is 1 inch wide and 12 inches long. Then cut it on the folded side as shown in the photograph and glue the uncut side to one edge of the cardboard. Do this on the other edge and then add bunches of narrow streamers, each about 1½ inches long, to the tops and bottoms of the loop and the stick.

When the glue is dry, play your hand drum by gently rolling the stick back and forth between your palms. The drum will make a patter as the erasers swing and strike the waxed paper.

FIESTA FOODS

Everyone loves *fiesta* foods. Like the *fiesta* itself, these foods, while traditional, are a spicy change from the regular meal of *frijoles* and *tortillas*. One of the favorites is a little chicken *taco*, which you can easily make. You will need *tortillas*, cooked chicken cut in small pieces, string (or you can use shredded cornhusks), cooking oil, chopped green onion, grated cheese, and hot sauce.

Wrap several pieces of chicken in a soft *tortilla*, and tie the package with string or a strip of cornhusk. Cook the *taco* in hot oil for several minutes until it is crisp and brown. Remove the string, and pack the *tacos* in a large *canasta* lined with towels. Serve by sprinkling chopped green onion, grated cheese, and mild hot sauce on top. You can buy prepared sauce, or make your own, following the recipe on page 108. You can also substitute beef or lamb for the chicken to make a meat *taco*.

Another popular *fiesta* food is roasted corn. Carefully pull back but don't remove the husks from some ears of corn. Take out the silk and replace the husks. Soak the ears in water for a short time before cooking them. Lay the corn on slow-burning coals for fifteen to twenty minutes, turning the ears frequently. You can also shuck the fresh corn and wrap it in aluminum foil before roasting. Like the *tacos*, the corn is taken to the *fiesta* packed in a large *canasta* with towels.

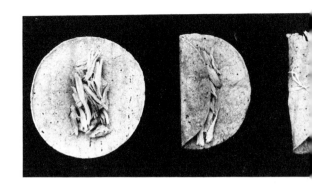

No *fiesta* or market would be complete without some kind of bean snack. The following one can be made with *tortillas*, mashed *frijoles* (see the recipe on page 107, and cream cheese. Cook soft *tortillas* in oil until they are crisp and flat. Spread some mashed beans on each *tortilla*, and on top of the beans, put a dab of cheese. For serving them at a *fiesta*, pack the crisp *tortillas* in a towel-lined *canasta*, and spread a *tortilla* with some *frijoles* and a little cheese for each hungry buyer.

Oranges are a familiar part of *fiestas*. They are sold from little carts that have a clever lathelike tool to remove the rinds. You will have to take the peels off by hand, or else leave them on, but the rest is easy. Cut the fruit in half and sprinkle the top with cinnamon and *chile* flakes or powder.

FLOATS

You might want to try making an airplane or tractor float like the ones in the photographs here and on the next page, or some other kind of bicycle-

powered float. How to build it will depend a lot on what shape you want to make and what kind of a bicycle you use.

Some of the materials you might find useful are chicken wire for structure, string, masking tape, crepe paper or construction paper, poster paints, and lightweight wire.

A PIÑATA

The breaking of a *piñata* is a familiar event in Latin America. You can make one in almost any shape you like—animals are very popular. A large balloon will serve well as a base for the body, and a smaller one for the head. Cover them with papier-mâché—strips of paper dipped in wallpaper paste—adding eight or nine layers of strips so that the forms will be very strong. It is best to let each layer dry before adding the next. Build in a loop at the top of the body—to string up the *piñata*—and leave a hole in the body through which you can fill it with candy. Legs, ears, tails, arms, etc., can be made using rolled newspaper or wire as bases and should be fastened to the body or head early, after the first four layers of papier-mâché have dried. You might want to use wire to attach them, and reinforce the joints heavily with papier-mâché. When the legs, ears, tails, etc., have been attached and are dry, continue adding four or five more layers of papier-mâché.

After these layers of papier-mâché are dry and hard, pop and remove the body balloon and fill the space with candy. Then cover the hole with layers of papier-mâché.

You can decorate your *piñata* with tissue paper, folded and cut into loops as for the hand drum, or with crepe paper. When it is finished, hang it up high somewhere until the time comes to break it. If you have built a good strong *piñata*, lots of people can take turns trying to break it. The person who is trying must be blindfolded and have a heavy stick. You can string your *piñata* anywhere you have enough room to swing a heavy stick safely. If you're at school, maybe you can string a rope between two poles and hang the *piñata* from the rope. This way the *piñata* can be raised and lowered as a person is trying to break it. It will fool him, and take longer to break the *piñata*.

GIGANTES

Every *fiesta* includes a wild dance by two pairs of 12-foot-tall *gigantes*. Everyone stops to watch and laugh, as the oversized figures waltz and sway. Special dancers stand inside the frames and work the mammoth puppets.

You can make *gigantes* in one of several ways. The simplest method is to use a lightly stuffed and painted paper bag for the head into which is inserted a coat hanger for the shoulders and a long pole or broom to hold the *gigante* up. You tape the coat hanger to one end of the pole, hang the dress from the coat hanger, and stand inside the skirt to hold the pole and make the *gigante* dance. You can use the directions on page 123 to make the dress.

If you want to make a wooden-framed *gigante*, like those in Guatemala, only smaller, you can follow these directions, which will give you a *gigante* about 8 feet tall.

Barefoot men work the 12-foot-tall *gigantes*.

Gather the following supplies:

4 pieces of 1- × 2-inch wood, 8 feet long (for the legs)

4 pieces of 1- × 2-inch wood, 25 inches long (for the braces)

1 piece of 2- × 4-inch wood, about 26 inches long (for the shoulders)

Glue

Small nails

String

Papier-mâché supplies

Long stick

Paint

Shellac

Yarn

Cloth

Pair of gloves

To make the body of the *gigante*, cut one end of each 8-foot-long piece of wood at a steep angle, as shown in the photograph. Your angles don't have to be too accurate. We used a saber saw and eyeball guesses, and it worked OK. These 8-foot pieces will be the legs of the frame. The slanted ends of the pieces should be glued and nailed to the 2- × 4-inch shoulder piece, as shown.

Brace the frame by attaching two of the 1- × 2- × 25-inch pieces to the legs, one to the front and one to the back of the frame. Attach them so that they are parallel with the shoulder piece and about 2 feet from the ground. The two other 1- × 2- × 25-inch pieces are to brace the sides and should be attached to the frame about 3½ feet from the ground. If you glue the braces

Top: The angles of the top ends of the legs
Bottom: The frame with legs and braces in place

in place, you will need to tie them at the right height until the glue dries.

Make the head a little larger than life-size out of papier-mâché. You can use chicken wire or wadded-up newspaper for a form. Before you begin applying your first layer of papier-mâché, secure a stout stick inside the form so that the stick protrudes about 1 inch through the top of the head and at least 6 inches from the bottom.

You can use poster paint to make the features on the face. When the paint is dry, cover it with a protective coat of shellac. Yarn would be good for the hair. Look at the photographs of the *gigantes* and borrow or make a hat you think will look well on yours. When the head and neck are finished, glue and nail the neck to the shoulder piece. Glue small bracing blocks to the shoulder piece, on both sides of the neck—this will make the neck stronger.

For both the male and female *gigante* a simple sacklike garment is used, and this can be stapled, glued, or tied to the shoulder piece. The arms are empty cloth tubes with large, stuffed gloves attached at the ends; they can also be stapled to the shoulder piece. The photographs of the *gigantes* may give you ideas for making the clothing.

There is a third possibility. If you can get an 8- or 10-foot aluminum stepladder you can use it for the frame of your *gigante*. With two pieces of wood tied at the sides, brace the ladder so that it stays open. Nail the head and neck to a wooden block and tie it to the top of the ladder. Dress the *gigante* by attaching the cloth to the wooden block. **DANCE!**

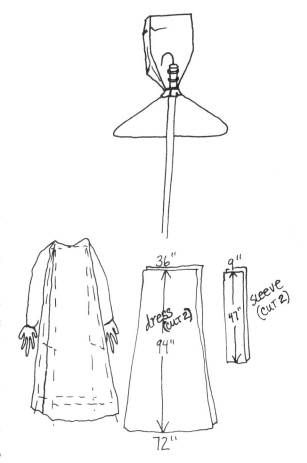

Afterword

You have just finished reading the main part of the book—you're at the end. We want to tell you how we felt about ending this book.

Beginning and writing the book were more fun than ending it. We felt alive and excited as each of us gave the other encouragement and ideas, criticisms and compliments. We learned about ourselves and about each other. We learned to be patient and to be careful. We learned to think about saying precisely what we meant. We wrote letters and talked to each other very often, and that was great.

It was hard for us to end the book, because it was a piece of work we'd loved doing. And it's hard to let something you love come to an end.

Vocabulary

You may find the simple guide that follows useful in pronouncing the Spanish words in the book. These are the sounds you would hear in Spanish-speaking parts of the Americas; in Spain the language is pronounced somewhat differently.

a   as in f*a*ther

b   as in *b*oy. V is pronounced the same way.

c   before a, o, u, as in *c*an
before e, i, as in *c*ity

ch   as in *ch*ina

d   as in *d*ay. Or *th* if the letter appears in the middle or end of the word.

e   as in p*ay*. Or as in l*e*t before or after a trilled r.

f   as in *f*an

g   before a, o, u or a consonant, as in go
before e, i, as in *h*en

h   silent, or as in *h*otel or *h*onor

i   as in d*ee*p

j   silent or as in *h*im

k   appears only in foreign words

l   as in *l*ong

ll   as y

m   as in *m*ay

n   as in *n*ot

ñ   similar to ny in ca*ny*on, but the sounds become one: niña (ni nya)

o   as in c*o*ne

p   as in *p*ay

q   as in *k*it

r   as in *r*ay, but trilled

rr   trilled more emphatically

s   as in *s*ir

t   as in pe*t* (use tip of tongue)

u   as in p*oo*l

v   as in *b*ay

w   appears only in foreign words

x   as in e*x*act. Except before a consonant, then as s in *s*tart.

y   as in *y*es

z   as in *z*one

adiós, good-bye

aeroplano, airplane

agua, water

ahora, now

ahorita, just now, in a little while

aire, air, wind

alcalde, mayor

amarillo, yellow

arco, rainbow

arroz, rice

atole, corn gruel, a thick cornmeal drink

auxiliar, an assistant, as for a mayor

ayudante, helper, assistant

azadón, broad-bladed hoe

baño, bath, bathroom

barrilete, kite

bien, good

blanco, white

bueno, good

café, coffee, coffee tree

cal, lime

canasta, basket

carpintería, carpenter's shop

cebollo, onion

cementerio, cemetery

centavo, cent

chile, pepper

chiles rellenos, a food made from peppers stuffed
with chopped meat and vegetables

chuchito, cornmeal and tomato-sauce snack

cinturón, belt

clase, class

cocina,   kitchen

comal,   pottery plate for cooking tortillas

comidas,   meals

cuando,   when

cuarto,   room

cuerda,   plot of land measuring 40 varas on each
  side

¡dele!,   signal for a bus to start

dia,   day

dormir,   to sleep

dueño,   owner

en,   in

enfermera,   nurse

escuela,   school

falda,   skirt

fiesta,   festival, celebration

flor,   flower

frijol,   bean

galera,   shed

gallina,   hen

gaseosa,   soft drink

gigante,   giant figure or puppet

gobierno,   government

gracias,   thanks

gringo, gringa,   foreigner

hombre,   man

huipil (Indian word),   Indian blouse

iglesia,   church

imagen, image

juego, game
juzgado, mayor's office and court

ladino, non-Indian
lejos, far

machete, large knife
maíz, corn
mañana, tomorrow, morning
mano, hand
matiosh (Indian word), thank you
marimba, a musical instrument
mercado, market
metate, stone on which cornmeal is ground
ministril, village official whose job is to keep order
molino, mill
mono, monkey
mucho, a lot, much
mujer, woman
muy, very

naranja, orange (fruit)
naranjo, orange tree
negro, black
niña, little girl
niño, little boy

padre, **father**
para, for
parque, park
parque central, central park
pasado, past

pepita, seed

petate, mat

pila, fountain with many basins

piña, pineapple

pitahaya, kind of fruit

plaza, public square

plazuela, small plaza

pollo, chicken

por, for

por favor, please

presente, present

profesora, teacher

puesto de salud, place of health, health clinic

¿qué?, what?

quehaceres, chores

queso, cheese

quetzal, bird, symbol of Guatemala. In Guatemalan money, a *quetzal* is a bill equal to one United States dollar in value.

quintal, approximately a hundred pounds

señor, Mr.

señorita, Miss

shak (Indian word), hello

sí, yes

taco, crisp tortilla snack

taller, workshop, factory

tiempo, time, weather

tienda, small store, shop

tomate, tomato

tortilla, corn pancake

trabajo, work

trompo, top (a toy)

tsute (Indian word),   carrying cloth

vara, measurement from center of chest to
    fingertips of outstretched arm, about a yard

y,   and
ya,   already, still

Index

About the Authors

Aylette Jenness and Lisa W. Kroeber have been close friends since they met in Cambridge, Massachusetts, in 1960. When they went to Guatemala to gather material for A LIFE OF THEIR OWN, they found that each brought to the project ideas and skills which complemented the other's.

Aylette Jenness has lived among peoples of different cultures in Alaska and Nigeria, and out of her experiences she has produced several distinguished photodocumentary books: *Along the Niger River: An African Way of Life* describes a multitribal area of northern Nigeria; *Dwellers of the Tundra*, about life in an Alaskan Eskimo village, was selected as an Honor Book in the 1970 Book World Children's Spring Book Festival. Lisa W. Kroeber has taught about Latin America in elementary schools for many years, and as a result, is well aware of what interests and motivates children. Her search for good readings and for activities related to Latin America has led her to develop an unusual set of curriculum materials for her students.

Aylette Jenness lives in Cambridge, Massachusetts, and Lisa W. Kroeber in Pacifica, California.